Sisters in Praise presents...

Journeys of Godly Women

Compiled by Jessica Robinson

EXPECTED END

E X

ENTERTAINMENT

Atlanta, GA, USA

Copyright © 2015 Sisters in Praise/Jessica Robinson

All rights reserved. No part of this book may be reproduced or transmitted in any form or by any means, electronic or mechanical, including photocopy, recording, or by any information storage and retrieval system with the exception of a reviewer who may quote brief passages in a review to be printed in a blog, newspaper or magazine without written permission from the author and/or publisher. Address inquiries to: Expected End Entertainment, P.O. Box 1751, Mableton, GA 30126.

Published by Expected End Entertainment/EX3 Books

ExpectedEndEntertainment@gmail.com * www.EX3ent.com

ISBN-10: 0996172203

ISBN-13: 978-0-9961722-0-2

Printed in the United States of America

DEDICATION

To Godly women all over the world. Your stories matter. You are unique and you are precious in the sight of God.
Psalms 139:14: *"I will praise thee; for I am fearfully and wonderfully made: marvelous are thy works; and that my soul knoweth right well."*

Contents

INTRODUCTION 1

JESSICA ROBINSON 3
    "She Shall Rejoice in Time to Come"

RAQUEL BRYAN 13
    "Living as Godly Women"

ANGIE LEWIS 23
    "I Will Not Be Job's Wife: Wounded Widow"

DR. CRYSTAL JONES 33
    "Alive. My Testimony About Life on Purpose"

MORRISSA NICOLE 39
    "Power"

SHINEKA KARIM 47
    "Becoming a Godly Woman"

JANELLE NUNES 53
    "He Has a Master Plan"

SARAH N.J. ANDERSON 63
    "Meeting the Master"

SHINNINE NEWMAN 71
    "What I Know Now"

RUTH NAOMI MITCHELL 77
    "Pure Gold"

KETURAH MORRIS 85
    "The Journey"

NASHARA PEART 91
    "I Will Never Forget the Day I Almost Lost My Mind"

SHARON EDMUND-BROWN 97
    "The Story Behind My Praise"

TRANESHA MARKS 105
    "You Can Win"

KANISHA ANDERSON 113
    "Lost and Found in the Balance"

ABOUT SISTERS IN PRAISE 123

ACKNOWLEDGMENTS

I must first acknowledge Jesus Christ, my Savior, my King, my joy, my peace, my love, my keeper, my hope, my salvation, my provider, my protection, my strong tower, my reason for living, and my burden bearer. Clearly, He is my everything and I owe Him my entire life because without Him I would be absolutely nothing. I am dependent on God like someone on life support. He is my life support. Secondly, I acknowledge the women who have contributed to this anthology. Many of these women have significantly contributed to my life and I want the world to know who they are. These women have been to hell and back and yet they are still standing. They are strong women who are pillars of strength. These women are Godly women!

Jessica Robinson

INTRODUCTION

Every journey has a destination. In preparation for our journey, we pack necessities and some, like myself, pack unnecessary items that causes luggage to be overweight at the airport. I am so serious about this packing thing that I bring an extra bag because I am certain they will tell me my bags are too heavy or close to it. I always feel like I need that extra skirt, that extra top, or those extra pairs of shoes. My thought process is: "I want to have enough clothes for every day and for every occasion." Ladies, you know what it is like to be underdressed; it's really a horrible feeling so we pack with the intent to avoid that.

Every journey comes with its ups and downs. If you travel by plane, you may experience turbulence or delays. Traveling by bus might take you a little longer to get to your destination. Road trips by car have their own set of circumstances, depending on your travel partners.

As in the natural, our spiritual journeys are filled with ups and downs, loads of things that we need to unpack, things that we need to pack, a few delays here and there, some turbulence, and oh, we cannot forget the good times.

Some may feel their bad days outweigh their good days, as if things just won't get better, and that expected end that Jeremiah speaks about in Jeremiah 29:11 is just unattainable. The reality is, every journey is unique, filled with different experiences, people, emotions, and growth.

This book contains 15 chapters from 15 women from different backgrounds, different life experiences, and different luggage. The one commonality is that they all have been saved by grace, washed in the blood of Jesus, and have found refuge in the King of Kings. The powerful thing about this book is that despite the different in places of origin, with different experiences along the way, we are all heading to the same place... heaven.

We may be at different points in our journeys, but we desire to hear, "Well done, thou good and faithful servant." We want to behold the power of His glory, look upon His face, be seated at the Masters table, and dance with our King. Why does this matter? It matters because this has been our strength during this journey. Many of us have been hurt, molested, abused, struggled with low self-esteem, confused with our sexuality, struggled with lust, fell into sexual sins, lost loved ones, and the list goes on and on. We have opened some of the pages of our lives to impact and inspire women all over this world. We pray that you are blessed by the words of this book.

Take this journey with us. Pray and fast with us. Discover the things that we needed to pack for our journeys, including faith, perseverance, and forgiveness, and see the baggage we needed to discard, such as suicidal thoughts, depression, and pain, so we could get closer to our destination.

We pray that you see yourself in some of our stories. We hope that you see how we overcame issues and circumstances that at times seemed impossible and that you accept the possible in your life. Enjoy the stories of strength and identity in Christ and join the journey of a group of Godly women.

SHE SHALL REJOICE IN TIME TO COME
BY JESSICA ROBINSON

I was 22 years old and praying to God about being single. Like most girls, I have always dreamed of being married, but I was dreaming about the wrong things. At 14, I had my first relationship with a young man who was significantly older. During this stage of my life, I did not take my Christian walk nor relationship with Christ seriously, so I simply did what I wanted to do.

My second boyfriend was a Christian. He was saved, anointed, spoke in tongues, and was one the most gifted musicians I had ever seen. And the boy could sing like an angel. I thought at 17 I had found "the one". You know, the one who made my heart skip a beat, the one who prayed with and for me, the one who sang to me, the one who texted me all day and all night, the one who made my heart smile. Again, I was wrong. Lucky number two was not the one for me. Usually after a bad break up, females tend to say, "I'm never doing this again", "That's it, I'm through", "These church guys, ugh!!", and then we simply repeat the cycle.

After my second relationship, which was a terrible break up, I said all of these things, but didn't enter a third relationship. However, I attached myself to men who I had no business attaching myself to. They were men who could seemingly be "the one" and fit my ideology of what I thought God wanted for me. I never dated any of them and nothing was official, but we hung out, spoke on the phone, laughed, talked, and did everything couples did without any type of commitment. The problem was I was creating soul ties with men who had no business being in my heart.

You're probably asking, "Well Jessica, why did you do it?" There are a number of reasons. I struggled with self-esteem issues so I stayed around these men who told me how beautiful I was, and other things I wanted to hear. I struggled with insecurity and these men made me feel "secure", important, and special. I had a void that I was trying to fill. I grew up without my natural father in my life, and as a young woman that is difficult to deal with. I did everything in my power to fill that void, but with the wrong things. I was searching for love in all the wrong places. Understand that during these times, I was in the church, worshipping God and singing on the choir. But I was in a place of shackles and chains because I had so many issues holding me down. It was a long and hard process but I made it through. When the last young man walked out of my life, it hit me like a ton of bricks, because I did not expect it. I had put so much into it and had gotten nothing out of it. I was devastated. Have you ever put so much into a relationship and got nothing out of it?

It was during this time of loneliness and devastation that I truly found the lover of my soul. I always loved Jesus and wanted to live for Him. My passion for the things of God allowed that to shine through, but I was walking around hurt, broken, shattered, and confused. I remember becoming free and allowing God to peel away the layers. It was like an onion. When you peel an onion, it has an effect on anyone in close proximity. This is how my life was being revealed. The day my process of healing and freedom began, it was truly a life-changing experience. I began allowing God to fill the empty areas of my life and love me like I needed to be loved. I allowed my heart to chase after Him, and seek Him first.

During this process, I went back to praying about my single life. As single women, we get frustrated in every sense of the word. We can be holy all we want, speak in tongues, and run around the church, but when we go home we are frustrated. We struggle with loneliness, we wonder if anybody will ever love us, and we wonder if we will ever be good enough to be someone's wife. My mom always made it her duty to tell me how beautiful I was, and how special I was. According to her, I was her princess, but isn't that what moms are supposed to say? Not having my natural father in my life and the complexities of my family created some very deep holes for me that only God could help me with. I remember going home crying, sobbing, depressed, sitting on the couch, and watching television wishing someone would call me or send me a text. I wanted someone to talk to. I was frustrated and became impatient. I was saying, "God I'm doing everything you are telling me to... praying, fasting, keeping myself pure, and seeking your face. So, can I have some companionship? Like for real, help a sister out over here! Please Jesus! Can I, please?"

Now, I cannot lie on God and say His answer was no but He did give me an answer as clear as day: "Serve like Ruth, with the heart of Esther. Pray like Hannah and wait like Sarah."

Immediately, I wrote it down. Sisters, when God spoke these words to me they brought me such peace and tranquillity. I stopped worrying and I started focusing on that current season in my life. God showed me that the single season in my life is a process, a critical process that I must go through. This process would enable me to be the woman of God he has called me to be to serve His people and to fulfil his plans for my life, in addition to being the Godly woman that my future husband will need to stand by his side in whatever capacity he serves. I want to specifically share this process of "Serving like Ruth". . .

Serving Like Ruth

When we speak of Ruth, most people assume it's in the context of her finding her "Boaz". But I am going to provide you with a different twist on the life of Ruth. I can relate to Ruth in many ways and I'm sure many of you can as well. Let us look at it from the angle of literally serving God rather than doing what we can so our future husband can see us. Ruth was a Moabite, not an Israelite. Moabites were descendants of Lot through incestuous relationships between Lot and his daughters, which can be referenced in Genesis 19:36-38. The Moabites were known for worshipping false gods, and making sacrifices to idols, which was of course unacceptable to God.

Ruth was also in the lineage of Jesus. Our Saviour came through a lineage of idol worshippers and other ungodly practices. It proves that God is able to turn any ugly situation into something beautiful.

So what does it mean to serve like Ruth? It means that as women of God, we need to serve God, serve God relentlessly and without apology. The reason why I brought up the linage of Ruth is because many people are held captive by their pasts. They cannot worship God in this "relentless" manner that I am talking about. Many women allow the enemy to plague their minds with where they used to be, even though they were delivered them from their past a long time ago. They are restricted in their prayer lives because each time they go down on their knees to pray, the enemy whispers to them about their past. Some women don't worship freely because they worry about their past and what people might say about them. There are other women who refuse to step out in ministry or do what God has called them to do because of their past, forgetting the new work that God has begun in them. However, Ruth did not allow this to be her story. I am sure that Ruth knew her background, her family life, and where she was coming from, but Ruth did not let this stop her as she stated these words to her mother-in-law Naomi, "Entreat me not to leave thee, or to return from following after thee: for whither thou goest, I will go; and where thou lodgest, I will lodge: thy people shall be my people, and thy God my God." (Ruth 1:16)

It is clear that Ruth was not going anywhere. I can imagine everyone talking about Naomi and pointing fingers and doing the same thing to Ruth. Not only did Naomi come back empty, but she brought back this false god serving, sacrificing to idols woman that her sons married.

Do you think Ruth knew that she was going to be in the lineage of Christ? The Saviour of the entire universe? I don't think so. What if Ruth decided to go home and allow her past to restrict her future? She would not have been such a significant part of history. What will you forfeit because you are allowing your past to dictate your future? It does not matter where you've been or what you've done, God is able to turn it around for your good. In Romans 8:28, it states: "And we know that all things work together for good to them that love God, to them who are the called, according to his purpose." When God says all things, He means all things, the good and the bad. I believe that the life of Ruth is a perfect example of Isaiah 61:3 - "to appoint unto them that mourn in Zion, to give them beauty for ashes, the oil of joy for mourning, the garment of praise for the spirit of heaviness; that they might be called trees of righteousness, the planting of the Lord, that he might be glorified." I believe that your life can be the very same. God will turn around every unfortunate circumstance and use it to bless someone else's life so that He can get the glory.

So what if you were abused, raped or molested, can God still use you? He sure can! So what if you used to be a prostitute, can God still use you? Yes He can and He will, if you allow him to. So what if you have children out of wedlock and their father is nowhere to be found? God can use you and He can use them. Each and every issue stated is a testimony of my own life and God has turned everything around for my good. Was it easy? No, it certainly was not. I struggled with insecurities, low self-esteem, depression, suicidal thoughts, and agnosticism. Ladies, I have been to hell and back.

There are many issues that I have never told anyone because I was embarrassed and ashamed. I am coming from abuse, molestation, and being raised in a single-parent household. There was a time when I was not rooted and grounded in God and my mind was attacked and I became agnostic, not knowing or understanding if God was real. I was 18, in my first year of college. I had just moved back to Toronto on my own. There was so much going on in my mind, my spirit, and my emotions. I was walking around wounded and I did not even know it. Talk about "dead man walking". I just wanted to die and throw in the towel. I could not feel God. It felt like His presence had left me and I was without hope. I remember telling Him to kill me and take my life because I didn't want to live like this anymore. That was the worst feeling in the world. I do not wish that feeling on anyone. I was wondering how atheist and agnostics lived without feeling anything, without being connected to God. It was the emptiest and darkest feeling that I have ever experienced and I can never go back there.

I also remember my mom telling my brothers and me stories of her sleeping with us in subway stations and being homeless. I was only four, but I remember it clearly. I remember my little black face on the cold concrete and being on the bus bundled up in my mother's arms along with my two baby brothers. I felt her struggle and pain. Even though I was only four, I felt like I needed to be strong for my mommy. I also remember my mother experiencing life-threatening domestic violence situations, where we all could have lost our lives. I felt it when he broke her legs. I remember her screaming. I remember him trying to drive the car over the bridge and kill us. I remember being 10 years old coming home to find my mother close to death and overdosed on a bottle of bills because she just could not take life anymore.

Although many of these memories are from 21 years ago, they continue to stain my imagination and sometimes my dreams. So, ladies, when I tell you that God can use you regardless of your past, I mean that from the core of my being. God can literally give you beauty for ashes. With everything I have been through, I never thought God would produce ministry and sermons out of it, but He did. Just like Ruth, each and every one of us has a story to tell and past that we have to live. But it is up to you to choose how you will allow your past to work for you. Don't allow your past to imprison you. It's sad to see so many women living in prisons because of their pasts. We can lay our issues at the feet of Jesus. Women of all ages, you can no longer allow these things to hold you captive and prevent your life from being a testimony. Paul says that it is by the grace of God that I am what I am, we all know that it is because of God's grace and mercies that we are here and no one else can get the credit. Many of us have been through situations that should have sent us to mental institutions, but we are still here and we are still here for a purpose and with a purpose. Say it with me, "*I am here for a purpose and with a purpose.*" Be the woman of purpose you were created to be. Don't be kept bound any longer.

Isaiah 54:16 states: "Behold I [God] have created the smith that bloweth the coals in the fire, and that bringeth forth an instrument for his work; and I have created the waster to destroy." I want you to focus on the phrase "that bringeth forth an instrument for his work". I remember the first time that stood out to me. I was blown away. Giving the verse that comes afterwards, "No weapon formed against me shall prosper," God showed me that everything that I have been through was an instrument to bring forth his work. All of that, God? Yes! All of that!

Woman of God, everything that you've been through is for a reason... to bring forth His work. The molestation, depression, suicidal thoughts, falling for temptations, history of promiscuity, all of that was an instrument for His work. God is famous for making something out of nothing. Look at man for example, God created man out of the dust of the earth. That is a revelation right there. God breathed life into him, gave him a name, and gave him dominion over all of the earth. With that being said, God can use your dirt and make something beautiful out of it. God can clean you up, turn you around and give you a new song in your heart. That is the kind of God that we serve.

In Genesis, the Bible says that the earth was without form or being but God said let there be and there was. God turned nothing into something. I can imagine God looking around saying, "I wonder what I am going to use to create man" and went ahead and used dirt. Of all the things God could have used, he used dirt. God could have simply called man into being. I mean He is God and He can do that. But He took the time out to use this dirt to form Adam. God is using your dirt to form you. God is forming you right now.

In 2 Cor. 5:17 it states: "Therefore if any man be in Christ, he is a new creature: old things are passed away; behold all things are become new." Woman of God, you are a new creature, a new woman, you are beautiful in the sight of God and oh how He loves you with an unconditional love. You have been reconciled with Christ through His blood and you have friendship with Jesus. The grace of God is covering you and His mercies are renewed every morning in your life. You must now feel like a lioness and like you can conquer the world. Look at your past and praise God for bringing you through.

Many times we hear that we have a purpose, but some of us do not believe it. It is time that we start believing that we were created for a purpose regardless of our upbringings and our past. Know that you are loved and highly favored of the Lord. The Bible refers to Mary, the mother of Jesus, as "blessed and highly favored of the Lord". Did you know that Mary was just a simple little girl that nobody knew? Yet, God chose to use her.

I want to end this chapter with one of my favourite scriptures, 1 Cor. 1:27 - "But God hath chosen the foolishness of this world to confound the wise; and God hath chosen the weak things of this world to confound the things which are mighty." Verse 28 continues to say that God chose the base things, and the things which are despised, so that God can get the glory. Now what does that tell you? It shows us that God is not looking for perfect people, otherwise He would not have gone to the cross to shed his blood. Again, we see that God is in the business of making something out of nothing. God chooses the nobodies, the runaways, the broken-hearted, the ones who have been molested, depressed, and suicidal. He uses every bit of us for his glory. Nothing is too bad, too stink much or too shameful for God to use. You were trash to someone else, but He made you his treasure, and you, His prized possession, are so marvellous in His sight. Also in 1 Cor. 9 it states, "Eyes hath not seen, nor ears heard, neither hath it entered into the heart of man, the things which God prepared for them that love him." This should offer so much consolation knowing that God has so much in store for you.

I am 100% sure that Ruth did not know her life would turn out the way it did. In Ruth 3:1, Boaz referred to Ruth as a virtuous woman. That is a strong title to add to anyone, and giving Ruth's past, how could she be called a virtuous woman? It is clear that Ruth's past was no longer an issue to worry about; it was just a foundation upon which her story was built. In the beginning of the book, they labelled her by her lineage "the Moabite" but by the end of the book, Boaz had no choice but to see Ruth beyond being a Moabite.

Woman of God, do not wear the label of your past anymore. I encourage you to serve God with everything in you and take a few pages, verses, and chapters out of the book of Ruth. Perhaps take some more time to study the life of Ruth and ask God to give you revelation on how you are able to live beyond your past like Ruth. It is not easy and it will take some work. One church mother said that "Something that took 15 minutes to break can take 15 years to fix." This is so true! Working through certain issues will and can take a lifetime. But more than anything, your healing comes from spending time with God and this is what I mean when I say serve God like Ruth. Boaz had nothing to do with this! God did all the work in Ruth's life and as a result Boaz was able to see the handy work of God. I pray that by reading this book you will no longer equate the life of Ruth mainly to Boaz, but will see how Ruth served God relentlessly and wholeheartedly in spite of everything she was encountering at that time.

Jessica Samantha Robinson currently resides in Toronto, Canada. She accepted the Lord Jesus Christ as her personal Saviour through baptism in the name of Jesus Christ at age 9, and received the gift of the Holy Spirit at 16. She is the eldest of three siblings. She was raised in the God-fearing home of Sharon and Damion Brown who taught her to pray and seek the face of God for herself. She attends the Triumphant Church of Jesus Christ (Apostolic) under the leadership of Bishop Evon Nunes. She serves as a youth leader at T.C.J.C, leads praise and worship, and sings on the choir.

SISTERS IN PRAISE

LIVING AS GODLY WOMEN
BY RAQUEL BRYAN

Living as Godly women today requires much work and sacrifice. This walk with Christ is not a sporadic nor momentary event. It is, however, an intentional daily process. Living as a Godly women entails so much that it's nearly impossible to describe in such few words. Nonetheless, I have tried to break it down in the next few pages. The intention of my thoughts being expressed are to empower you in understanding that it is very possible to survive and even thrive as a Godly woman in today's society. As a matter of fact, we should be doing just that. The world needs to see that Godly women are real people that struggle and fail at times, but can still be successful in all areas of our lives. Don't get me wrong, the appeal to things of the world will be there and the temptations will surely present themselves. But our vigor and passion to live for Christ as well as our hope and belief in Him must supersede it all.

Most of my journey as a child of God consisted of my making real faith-founded decisions. I remember at one point I knew I did not have the funds to pay my tuition. Things had not gone as planned and it was a really rough time for my family. Everything seemed to be a disaster in my life. I only had God to lean on. I would strategize how I would get the necessary funds. At one point, I legitimately stopped worrying. I pushed everything to the back of my mind just to get a little bit of peace. It was simply a coping mechanism to try and block out everything that was happening.

I went to church one Sunday night and the worship was so amazing. The minister began to prophesy that it was the appointed time to give a sacrificial offering. He prophesied that God was about to give us back a double portion and perform miracles in the lives of those who gave. Although he had prophesied on several different occasions concerning many different circumstances, I felt such a great personal connection with this particular prophecy. I knew I was not working nor was I expecting to start consistent employment due to my hectic school schedule but I just felt the urge to give unrestrained. There was one thing I could never argue; God has/had always been so faithful to His promises even when my faith wavered. That night I didn't second-guess the prophetic unction. I dug into my purse and pulled out my card to contribute a real sacrificial offering. I heard the Holy Spirit suggest the figure and I didn't even bat an eyelash at the sum. I went and I put the offering in the plate with complete belief in the power of God. I honestly had no clue what God was going to do but I knew it was going to be mind-blowing. The spirit of God was so thick in the service that I knew all He required was a leap of faith.

Later that week, the Holy Ghost told me to check my school email (mind you, I rarely check that email). In my mind, I kept asking "why"? I decided to check it just in case a professor had sent me an urgent message. The next few moments of the story still have me shaking my head in complete astonishment. As I scrolled down deleting some unimportant emails, I stumbled across one from the school. I was glad to see it was a recent email as a late reply to an urgent message could have created an issue. I opened the email. I couldn't believe my eyes! I had to read the email several times to make sure that it was not a daydream. The school informed me that they were offering to pay half my tuition with no repayment needed. Saints and brethren, fellow readers, if there was one time when I knew God to be amazing, this was it! All I could do was prostrate in worship and thanksgiving as I was so moved with emotion and gratitude at how God had used my faith to grant me what I needed. I was floating on clouds and walking around with a plastered smile on my face for days! This story will forever remain a part of one the chapters in my Christian journey to simply remind me that GOD CAN. Faith is just the bridge for Him to work in our lives.

Balance

As a passionate person, it's so easy to give much of my time to one thing and give it 100%. I have certainly learned that while that is necessary, we must also have balance. It is not healthy for one to be unstable or so driven in one area while completely neglecting another. This was a lesson I learned. I would be so focused on church and ministry while overlooking my responsibilities at home, at school, in relationships, at work, or simply habits surrounding my personal wellbeing. The same balance is also necessary for any other area of my life. It became a daily practice and regular evaluation to reinforce balance in my life.

As a single lady, it would seem that I have all the time in the world since I don't have a child or husband to center my life around. But I was often so preoccupied with so many different tasks and ministries. Sometimes I became cumbered with the responsibilities of the ministry that I ended up serving the ministry rather than the God of the ministry. We must take all necessary steps to maintain good physical and spiritual health. I have learned that it is so important that we never neglect personal time with God whether in prayer, meditation or worship. The success of this Christian walk and effectiveness of our ministry depends heavily on it. Prayer taught me so much about the need for balance and thoughtful change in so many parts of my life.

Prayer

What can prayer do for me, some may have asked or are still asking? If there is one thing I've learned over these last few years is the POWER of PRAYER. Can you just give faith in God and his promises a try? Prayer is that basic concept that allows the weakest of persons an opportunity to enter into communication with God. I recall so many times where all I could do was fall to my knees in tears. I would share my thoughts with God and He would always have a word of comfort or empowerment to share. There were also times when I struggled to pray. It was a constant battle to have successful prayer times but the key was to keep pushing until something happened. Prayer gives you an unlimited and priceless access to God. I don't write this as one who has mastered in this field but I write this as someone who knows the benefits and genuinely strives to grow constantly in this area.

I'll share a testimony with you. For the protection of this person, I will use the name Bob. One day, I was sitting at home working profusely at some assignments. I heard the Holy Ghost say stop what you're doing and get in to prayer. At that time, I had no idea why I was prompted so intently but I had this unquestionable and unavoidable impression in my spirit to get on my knees and speak to God. Might I just stop here to add, it is so important to live a spirit-led life. I am not saying I am always there as many times I drift from the level I need to remain but after this experience I was certainly thankful to God that I was living in the Spirit at that moment.

So we continue... I knelt down and I began to give thanks and praise to God like it was going out of style. My worship led into deep intercession for many and then it happened. I began to pray with a whole different level and intensity. The Holy Spirit had now led me to pray for Bob. I heard the Lord say, "Rebuke and curse cancer in his life." It was almost as if I was outside my body watching all this happen. As I concluded the prayer, I heard the Holy Ghost say, "Call Bob." I honestly didn't think anything of it so I gave him a call. As he picked up the phone he said, "You would never believe that I'm just leaving the doctor's office after what they believed was going to be terrible news." Of course I was extremely stunned because that was certainly not what I was expecting to hear at the beginning of a conversation. I allowed him to continue. Bob said that he was at the doctor to complete some procedures but upon completing the procedures and receiving the results, the doctors were amazed as they had expected the worst. He was cancer free! I was so moved by the words that all I could do was cry. I had no clue that the doctors had even suspected cancer but the Holy Ghost was ahead of the game. That is only one of the real examples that leads me to defend the power of spirit-led prayer.

If there is one thing I can confidently say, you have the power to change things through prayer. Women, you have what it takes to touch God. I often think of Hannah who couldn't even find the words to say but called out to God from her spirit. She had surpassed the surface and dug deep into the heart of the matter. She needed a child and was going to seek God despite what her enemies had to say. Even those that were in high places thought she might be crazy. That was how fervent and intense she became in seeking God. It was at that point when her prayer became her meat. Needless to say, God heard the desires of her heart and had to move on her behalf. Her fervency attracted God's attention.

Sisters in Praise, led by our faithful leader, Jessica Robinson and our team, amazingly emphasizes and dissects the aspects of prayer in seeking God until we hear from Him. I have certainly been a beneficiary of the results from this group. There are many times when I was hurting deep inside or just couldn't find what it took to seek Christ on my own and this group of praying sisters led me into a place of prayer. Some mornings when I had to speak, I had no clue what I would bring to the people nor was I confident in my ability to do so but God came through for me. The prayer group has grown immensely both in numbers but also in spiritual force against the enemy and in the independent development of each participant. For this, I am undoubtedly and forever grateful.

Moments of intense and effective prayers are precluded from unrehearsed, free and passionate worship experiences. I've proven the levels of change experienced from deep unrestrained worship lead me to a place of complete brokenness. It leads us to a place where we see the issues within ourselves rather than the problem with everyone else. It's those times of real brokenness that God reveals where we can grow, unlocks our gifting, buttresses our mantle, unveils our future, and heals us from our deep hidden secrets that may have been keeping us stagnant. Best of all, it is at this moment of brokenness that we are the closest and most intimate with Christ. Prayer has and will forever play such a key role in my journey as a Christian woman because it's one of the Christian practices that is guaranteed to work every time. Prayer was what kept me from staying in a backslidden state and throwing in the towel. Prayer is what kept me from following my siblings back into the world when that could have been "the easier" road. Prayer was and has been my lifeline.

Intercessors, even as I write, I am moved with convicting emotions. We cannot afford to drop the ball or leave our posts. Prayer and fasting won't always be attractive to our flesh but we must continue with our mantle. Someone's life, dreams, hope, health, protection and spiritual wellbeing depend heavily on the work we do.

Dedication & Commitment

It's a mind thing! When you know your identity, it surpasses the clichéd expectations. You move past what people have to say. It takes overlooking the fact that some people will call you crazy or even extra. Living this Christian journey is an intentional choice to live for God. As Godly women in the 21st Century, sometimes we are brought into "wilderness experiences" because there's an element of pruning that happens in the various stages of our lives. For me, I felt that people were just looking at me as the one who had it all together and the one who was too God-centered. This almost caused me to retreat and slow down my passion to please people. One day, I just remembered thinking, God I can't do this anymore. This is just who I am. I can't just chill. I refused to stifle my passion and excitement for the things of God. My dedication and commitment was part of my journey that I could no longer afford to subdue. So, I chose to just be free being who I was because I couldn't chose others over who I knew I was supposed to be in Christ.

In closing, I'll share one more, quick story of part of my journey which really shaped my identity as a young woman of God. My memory was brought back to a changing point in my life. I had sought the Lord about my post-secondary choice. I knew attending a university with no church in the area was not an option. I was not willing to become lukewarm or backslide and I really felt that going to a city that did not have a fire-filled church would lead me down that path. As a result, I had planned to forward my application to continue my post-secondary schooling to two universities. Somehow, (which now I can look back and see that it was all God as I never forget such important dates), I completely missed the date to apply to one of the schools. I was so devastated and frustrated with myself. I legitimately now had all my eggs in one basket. To make a long story short, I was so sure in my spirit that I took a leap of faith and signed a lease in Hamilton without even being accepted to McMaster University. I just knew that was where God wanted me to be. As I signed the paper, I remember saying, "God this is all you now."

As I was driving back to Toronto, I got an email from the office of the registrar stating that I had been accepted into one of the programs I applied to. Mind you, prior to accepting my offer of admission, I requested that God fulfill three specific things as a means of confirming His will. I never uttered any of these required confirmations from my mouth until the entire process was over. I was still waiting on the second confirmation to happen and sure enough the following week I was accepted to the program I desired. I was still in high anticipation because I was still waiting on the third confirmation. I called the school to see if all of my credits, almost two years of them, would be transferred to McMaster. The lady went completely silent on the phone and began stuttering stating that in all her years working in that position, she had never seen credits in that volume transfer completely. She re-checked several times to make sure that she had not overlooked anything. Amazingly, all my credits were transferred! It was at that moment that I broke down into tears because the entire situation just proved that God was so real to me. Until this day, so many are in opposition with my choice to leave my hometown. Prior to my moving, I cried every day for two weeks because people had turned against me, family members nagged me and many spread rumors about my reasons for leaving. Although I was confident that it was God's choice for my life, I felt like those closest to me turned away and did not trust God's plan for my life which left me feeling broken and alone. Not only was I venturing out away from everything I knew, I was also taking financial leap on my own.

Today, I can honestly say that I can see how God's hand has been on my life. Tears come to my eyes as I write because I know that God had me move to an unfamiliar place, which I initially hated, to grow. I could have never dreamed of half the experiences, changes, lessons or opportunities if I hadn't let go of my "perfectly planned out" life and let God's will become my next move. Moving to Hamilton has shaped my identity as a friend, employee, sister and child of God. The journey has consisted of much turbulence but also so many lifetime relationships that have caused me to grow immensely and life-changing experiences that never would have happened had I not moved. The demands on my spiritual gifts, positions in ministry and relationships have made me into the young lady I am today. I sincerely say, I do not regret it at all. Every experience, pain, tear, heartbreak, laugh, relationship, moment of failure, and worship experience has added to building my resolve to serve Christ even more.

There are so many other areas to cover when speaking about Godly women but I wanted to express my thoughts on some of the fundamentals and life experiences in this journey. If I should leave you with a thought it would be this: To be a Godly woman in this world, we require an undying love for God, which develops through an unwavering conviction of our sole reliance on Him. This love will lead to faith and this faith will lead to trust. The trust will lead to sacrifice and the sacrifice will lead to commitment and the commitment will lead to impact. In sum, being a Godly woman in the 21st Century requires that above all, we are agents of light and change in a world where the true expression of the love of God is in high demand. We must not be afraid to share our unique stories because these stories can change a life, strengthen the weak and build our faith.

Raquel K. A. Bryan was born in Toronto, Ontario. She now resides in Hamilton, Ontario, where she attends Apostolic Ark Ministries under the leadership of Bishop K. L. Morris and Co-Pastor P. Morris. She has completed her Honours Bachelor in Sociology and a certification in Small Business and Entrepreneurship. She is currently a student at the University of Toronto where she aims to complete her

Bachelor of Education. Raquel embraces the company of her family and friends as well as hobbies like sports, writing, singing, reading, song writing and traveling. Raquel also serves as an executive member on the Sisters in Praise board.

SISTERS IN PRAISE

"I WILL NOT BE JOB'S WIFE!"
WOUNDED WIDOW
BY ANGIE LEWIS

It all started with a headache. After a joyous and blessed afternoon at church, we settled in at home to relax the rest of the day and potentially return for another outpouring of God's goodness at evening service. Our family was small but beautiful. Mark and I were married for five beautiful years, with a 2-year-old daughter and one on the way (5 weeks to be exact). His eldest daughter was also a part of our growing family. We loved the Lord and were involved with ministry in several capacities. Juggling this, along with our careers and entrepreneurial efforts, did not reduce or minimize our availability to be content with our life at home.

I'd noticed that Mark wasn't in the best of spirits and wasn't as energetic that Sunday evening, he simply wanted to rest for the week ahead. I couldn't blame him, but for him to miss church was kind of odd. I, however, pressed my way to church, nine months pregnant and all. I remember my testimony quite vividly: I was giving God thanks for this second pregnancy because God has shown me the meaning of faith, persistence and strength in the midst of all what I was facing. As a result I revealed our expectant daughter's name "Hannah Faith", simply because God's faithfulness has proven true yet again by blessing us with another child. Mark prayerfully selected this name that would forever mark our child's destiny and calling. I also thanked God for what He was about to do in my life by declaring that I know the future may or may not be in my favor, but it was in God's favor. I had no idea what I was saying, but my testimony was a preliminary to what would have been the hardest and challenging days of my life.

Fast forward to that Friday, July 24, 2009. It was one day following Mark's annual checkup and a suggested CAT scan to pinpoint the reasons for his recent frequent headaches. Around 3 am, he said his headaches got more intense, and he had to vomit. I followed him to the bathroom where he did vomit as I rubbed his back. He looked at me with a terrified and nervous look and said, "I love you, baby." I was confused but I was quite sure he knew something was wrong with him, something that I had yet to experience, endure, process and overcome. I said, "I love you, B," and continued rubbing his back until he was through, and cleaned up.

That morning I did not sleep. I watched him as he had intermittent sleep, waking up every 10 minutes or so to cry out in pain, then drifted back to sleep. He and I ran a radio show for our church and in the midst of being in pain, he assured me that I could handle it alone. I called in to do the show so I could remain at home to keep an eye on him. Afterwards, he instructed me to go to work, which was five minutes away, and he would try to sleep off his headache. Reluctantly, but in obedience, I made my way to work.

About one hour into working, I received a call from our Primary Care Physician, who had an urgency in her voice. She asked me where my husband was. When I said home, she ordered me to get him to the closest hospital immediately. I panicked, breaking into a cold sweat, when she said the results of his CAT scan were not good. I immediately called on the name of Jesus. I called my hubby and told him to get ready to go to the hospital, rushed home and we headed to there.

Our walk from the car into the emergency room was long, symbolic and eerie. I led the way, with his hands on my shoulder as we slowly walked through the sliding doors. I never knew that once we walked through those doors, I would have entered the beginning of the hardest days of my life, and the last of his.

Wounded Widow

Upon checking him into the emergency room, we were met by a fleet of South Florida's top neurosurgeons and brain injury specialists. Some were there to tend to the issue at hand, and some were there in awe. I learned that his condition resulted from a tangled web of veins and arteries that spontaneously ruptured in the subdural part of his brain. This all means that it was unexplainable, unforeseen, and not caused by any external or internal factors or signs. I remember watching him writhe in pain, asking me to tell him what the doctors were telling me, and I was speechless. All I could do was hold his hand and rub his chest. Somehow, in the midst of all the pain and confusion, my husband encouraged me to stay strong, whispered a prayer for me and made me laugh. My God, what a man!

After calling immediate family members, pastors and colleagues, I went to the restroom to pray and declare some things. I knew this was going to be an extremely difficult situation. I slammed the bathroom door behind me, looked at myself in the mirror and said, "I will NOT be Job's wife! I will NOT be Job's wife! I will NOT be Job's wife!"

I still don't know why I said that. All I know is that I was staring in the face of a very sick man, surrounded by intrigued and puzzled nurses and physicians, nine months pregnant, with a 2-year-old at home. My integrity was being challenged. Everything was being tested, including my faith, my home, my lifestyle, my livelihood, and most of all the love of my life was going through. There was no way I was going to buckle, break or back down, and curse God, or influence my husband to.

I felt the urge to build up my spiritual reinforcement by preparing myself for what lied ahead. I don't recall uttering a prayer, but those six words is what echoed in my mind, body and spirit as I slowly absorbed what was happening in that emergency room. As I exited, I was met by my Bishop and several members who came with him. They immediately began praying and encouraging us, which was much needed. At that moment, I was told that the results of the CAT scan were inconclusive. It was either a large bleed on the brain that was in fact growing, or it could be an unusually large brain tumour giving off fluid. The only way that it can be successfully identified and dealt with, is by conducting a craniotomy, which is an invasive brain surgery, locating it and conducting whatever is necessary to control or eliminate it.

I stood there in shock, unable to move and unable to process what was being said. He had to repeat himself several times, and each time it became more and more unbearable. Then I began to slowly connect the dots, so to speak. My husband, my best friend, provider, the father of my children, lover and business partner was now having to undergo an invasive brain surgery that may or may not help him, and may also come with life-long debilitating effects. Repeat that again, Doc?

Approximately 48 hours later, while at home with our immediate family that started to trickle in from all over, I received a phone call from the hospital. They were unable to control the swelling in Mark's brain, and would have to conduct the craniotomy sooner than expected. My verbal consent was needed immediately. I nervously gave the consent and headed to the hospital. This was a Sunday morning and our usual routine of getting dressed and prepared for church. Surprisingly, on the way to the hospital, I somehow found myself at church. I walked through the doors, just in time for corporate prayer, and asked the church to pray for Mark. The wave of prayer was immediate, intense and passionate, as church members, friends and even visitors began calling on the name of Jesus to heal, deliver and cover my husband. The strength received as I felt the words being uttered travel and take effect on the situation at hand. A few members choose to be with us during surgery, which was kind and much needed.

We made it just in time for him to be rolled out, and I was ecstatic to see, touch and kiss him before surgery. With his eyes closed, he said, "Bee, you all right?" All I could do was smile and say, "Yes, Bee, I'm good." He was always selfless in nature and in thought, always looking out for the wellbeing of others before himself, especially in the most crucial of times. Before the orderly had to take him into surgery, I was given a prayer cloth from his childhood friend who is a renowned preacher and prophet. I was only instructed to hand it to him. But Mark took it, put it on his forehead and said, "In the name of Jesus, I will come out all right." I smiled and told him I loved him. He said he loved me too, and was taken to the operating room. From that moment on, I knew without a doubt, our lives would never be the same!

The Days Ahead

The days following his surgery were scary, at times unbearable and emotional. We expected the recovery to be difficult but it was very volatile with the successful removal of hematomas and burst blood vessels to him being unresponsive, heavily lethargic, and partially comatose. Through it all, I had to be there in physically, mentally and spiritually. I had to be the executor and inquirer of all his medical procedures. I had to question all the activities and make notations of all of the medications given and the necessity of them all. I had to make sure the staff knew that I was involved, interested, concerned and serious about my husband's wellbeing and ultimate recovery.

I was at times asked not to stay as late or come as early since I was in the last weeks of pregnancy and I needed to focus on my unborn child and my health. Of course, I didn't listen and was even more aggressive with my stance as his wife and number one supporter. About the fifth day after surgery, there was a major turnaround. Mark was still heavily sedated but his spirit wasn't. We got visitors in droves. Even with his eyes shut, he was able to identify, speak to, laugh with, tell jokes, and most importantly, pray for those who visited him. Again, God blew my mind and so did Mark. This man was resilient in spirit and character, and his spirit man would not sleep.

He told me that he wanted his audio KJV Bible on constant rotation in his room, and I made sure of it. Watching him pull through in slow and steady strides gave me the push I needed to continue on and be the woman he needed me to be, not only to him but to our children.

Folks had the tendency to call me strong, amazing, loving and unbelievably poised about the whole situation. They could not believe that I would have a smile on my face most of the time, and even participate in the jovial banter Mark would almost always initiate. I still don't see what they were talking about, because no one knew of the nights when I would buckle at the doorway of my house to my knees, have crying fits and tantrums, take hour long showers while crying out to God, and asking Him why? No one knew the sleepless nights where my eyes fixated on the ceiling or any inanimate object just to stop me from thinking or feeling what was happening to my husband and my family. I don't think many knew of the spiritual attacks that took place on my body and mind from forces so dark and sadistic that I could smell their stench as they lingered around me. I literally heard growls, snarls and raspy breathing as I laid down, or as I drove or tried to pray or do anything remotely functional. The fight was extremely intense, spiritually, and it took a toll on me, but many instead saw the unwavering strength and content face of Angie Lewis-Evans who refused to be Job's wife. I refused to be identified as one who limited, discredited or deemed the God of all heaven and earth incapable of doing the miraculous and impossible. Not I.

Somehow, I was energized and ready to tackle, question, approach and even initiate the absolute best of my husband's care. As a woman who was loved, spoiled, cared for and admired by an amazing man of God, I did not consider it a task or a strain to make sure I fulfilled my vow and duty to love him in sickness and in health. I was just doing what every wife would do, or should do.

Daddy's Home!

August 24, 2009, exactly 30 days after his admittance to the emergency room, Mark was on his way home! He eventually left the general observation, and was transferred to a rehabilitation centre to regain the strength of his left eyelid, hand and leg; ensure his cognitive and perceptual abilities; and work on any other challenging factors caused by the hematoma and surgery. I gave birth to our second daughter on August 14th. It was God's mercies and grace since my doctor could not comprehend how Hannah and I survived such a stressful period and postnatal ordeal.

Mark had only been in the rehab for two weeks but had made significant strides in improvement. I was unable to see him for five days since I had to give birth, but I pushed my way to see him three days after having our daughter. I even brought her along so he could meet her. When he saw me, he stood up for the first time and walked towards me. When he met Hannah, his smile lit up the lobby. I knew I was breaking every medical rule in the book as it pertained to newborns, but I had to let him hold her. He cradled her perfectly, and whispered in her ear something only the two of them know, then looked at me and thanked me for bringing his 'Kitten'.

He walked through our front door, unassisted on August 24, 2009! Hallelujah! God be praised! I felt the presence of God stronger than ever. As he walked in, I stood behind him and waved my hands in gratitude for what the Lord had done this far in our lives. It indeed was a testimony of God's faithfulness and the miracle He had performed. I had my family together again, and it felt oh so right! The doctor appointments, follow up therapy sessions, and necessary checkups seemed insignificant and paled in comparison to the joy of having him with us yet again. We witnessed him strive, regain strength and even drive again all in time. Then the beginning of destiny started to take place.

Daddy's Gone Home!
About six weeks after his return home, we noticed some changes in Mark's eating pattern, and he was losing strength. I started to question his neurosurgeon, and other specialists of what might be happening. I was reminded of the possible effects of the brain injury and surgery. We were told of possible organ failure. Mark took this grim but manageable prognosis in stride. He refused to let it totally diminish his quality of life, and his ability to be a husband and father to his family. He managed to set up Hannah's swing, assemble Melody's play kitchen, cook for me, and even make it to church a few Sundays. His love for God in the midst of all this at times dumbfounded me and had me questioning my own personal relationship with Him.

In late October, we planned a grand reception following Hannah's dedication, which also served as a victory dinner for Mark. We did it in fine style by renting a catering hall, getting colour coordinated elaborate wall decorations, favours and cutlery. This was catered to perfection by friends and family. I incorporated a general "thank you" to everyone that stood by us, assisted in any way and offered up countless prayers and well wishes. It was beautifully set up.

Unfortunately, everyone enjoyed the evening except Mark. That evening on his way to the reception, he was not feeling well and had to go to the emergency room. That day was bittersweet because we celebrated our daughter's dedication to the Lord, were surrounded by family and friends, but missed the presence of the honoree.

This admission to the hospital was unfortunately his last, because on Saturday, at 1:20 pm November 7, 2009, five days before his 42nd birthday, the Lord called Mark home to rest. That day was surreal and extraordinary. I remember waking up feeling a weird movement in my stomach as if something was being removed. I could see my husband's face flash before my eyes, and I knew at that very moment, he was preparing to leave me. Within that moment, the hospital called that his vitals dipped dramatically and that they believe their efforts are becoming futile. I was then faced with making a dreadful decision of whether or not to remove him from life support. After all conclusive tests have proven that his vitals were only as a result of the medications coursing through his body and the ventilator, I painfully signed off on the disconnection. I asked for time for us to say our farewells and for my pastor and others to make it to the hospital.

I vividly remember walking into that room, watching him rest peacefully, surrounded by an army of machines, tubes and medication. I immediately greeted him as if he would respond by saying, "Hey Honey, good morning!" I then took him by the hand and told him how much I love him, how much he's loved me and changed me as a woman. I was honoured to be his wife and the mother of his children and thanked him for choosing me to go on this amazing journey. I also told him that I thanked him specifically for giving me two little girls who look exactly like him, despite doctors saying it was impossible for me to have children. At that moment his already low vitals did a mild spike and deflection, as if he acknowledged all that I was saying. I smiled and continued to appreciate and honour him for being an example of change, as he gave his life to the Lord only five years earlier and had become a role model to all he came in contact with. I held his hand in solidarity acknowledging that this was in fact the end of our journey together as husband and wife.

I even called my children and had them acknowledge that their daddy was going to heaven. This was indeed painful to do, but I felt it necessary to be done.

I was honoured to have my Priest/Covering/Husband Mark Anthony Evans in my life for the last 8 years, 5 of them in Blissful Holy Matrimony. He fought the good fight, kept the faith, and Glorified God all the way. 11/7/09 @ 1:20pm is when the Heavenly Reception began. Hallelujah!! "I didn't leave you, I'm waiting for you." (Angie Lewis-Evans Facebook post: November 7, 2009).

Many women who have become widows whether thru a long battle with illness, or suddenly and unexpectedly, all have experienced the same level of pain, loss and emptiness. This is regardless of our religious beliefs or social status. The experience of death is unexplainable once you've experienced the intense love of a spouse.

After Mark's burial, there were also days of spiritual satisfaction when I was reminded of his heavenly reward. But those days of severe anxiety, anger, pain, anguish, bewilderment and carelessness took root too. If it were not for my children, I would have given up on life a long time ago, and would have been a woman void of life, purpose and drive. There were days when I wished the people who said: "You're so strong, stay strong, be strong, think strong…" would just shut up! I did not want to be strong, or show myself as being able to raise two toddler girls alone as mother and father! That was not what I wanted to do.

But somehow, along the way, in the midst of that storm and difficult transition the spirit of God made intercession for me. He became my judge and defender, and my children's father. He lived for me, when I didn't want to live. He carried me when I didn't want to be carried, and the love of God loved me when I felt unlovable and hopeless.

In this, I intentionally focused on the relationship my late husband had with Christ because it was his relationship with the Lord that convicted me each and every time I wanted to give up and give in. His intentions towards me and our girls was what motivated me to get up on the days I wanted to lay down and die. I aspired for more, aimed higher, and provided by God's grace and also by Mark's infallible inspiration and devotion towards his family.

As a woman who was widowed at age 28, there were a lot of things in life that I inadvertently missed out on. I was left to face harsh conditions, unfavourable treatment and difficult words from those who used to be loyal and true friends. I learned to regain my footing and balance in every aspect of life. I learned the art of forgiveness, which freed me in so many ways and gave me the ability and strength to love, laugh, live and strive.

I learned to fully embody the resistance of refusing to become Job's foolish wife when I no longer was Mark's wife. His illness and subsequent transition, catapulted me into a realm of despair and nakedness, but that was temporary when I learned to refocus and understand where the source of Mark's love for me came from... Christ.
I hope this piece inspires, enlightens, and strengthens women who have gone through inexplicable losses in life. Be encouraged and believe that in loss, death or deduction, God can and He will be all that we need to survive. It is in Him that we live, move and have our being. I am a testimony of bouncing back, bruised and all, but nonetheless I had the buoyancy to bounce, all because of Christ.

Angie Lewis (formerly Evans) is a mother of two beautiful daughters, Melody-Grace and Hannah-Faith. She resides in New Jersey and is a director for an alternative staffing agency for individuals with disabilities and other barriers. She loves the Lord Jesus Christ and is aiming every day to be more like Him. She's the widow of the late Bro. Mark Evans, who in only 5 years of salvation, made an indelible mark on the body of Christ with his contribution and desire to learn and share the Word of God. Angie is dedicated to being an advocate for widows, the fatherless and less fortunate.

ALIVE. MY TESTIMONY ABOUT LIFE... ON PURPOSE
BY DR. CRYSTAL JONES

"And be not conformed to this world: but be ye transformed by the renewing of your mind, that ye may prove what is that good, and acceptable, and perfect, will of God." – Romans 12:2

"In all thy ways acknowledge Him and He will direct your path." – Proverbs 3:6

Never did I, for even the slightest moment, think that being touched by 'him', one of the few men that I could trust, would have any impact on me. I respected him, so what he forced me to do had no ability to have an impact on me for the rest of my life. I rationalized it. It became normal. The only thing that wasn't taken was my virginity.

Years and years went by. I was sexually promiscuous in the tenth grade; that's what I had to give. That's what I grew to know. I was the good girl to most. To a few, I was known as 'his' girlfriend that was down for whatever. I became addicted to perpetuating the cycle of doing what was necessary to appease men that I felt comfortable with. Still, unaware of the seed planted, I thought I was just addicted to the pleasure, until I decided that no longer would a man control me physically.

Then there was 'her'. I allowed the idea of being equal with a woman control my life for seven years. Love was love.

Not too many knew since I grew up the daughter of a preacher and that was unacceptable. On campus, I fought to be accepted. I will forever be grateful for a best friend who never accepted less than my best. He would call and pray and hang up. I rationalized it. He told me that it would not always be like this. I just wanted him to accept me. He never did. He believed for me and I'm forever grateful!

In the midst of those seven years, my addiction to alcohol and drugs began. I hated my reality so I chose to consistently live in another reality. I could never do the same drug two days in a row because I had a fear of being addicted. If I was addicted, my 4.0 GPA would no longer cover my scars. I drank heavy on the weekends as that was normal for college life. No matter what, I needed to be out of my reality. I had given the first "her" three years of my life and someone decided that she would take my place. Anger filled my heart as I reached around and watched her become increasingly lifeless. Never would someone take from me that which was mine. I did not care about my life so I surely did not care about hers. The same night, I decided that I would slit my wrist. Taking pills carried the possibility of not taking enough, hanging myself would hurt too much and jumping from the third floor could simply end in an injury. This could not happen with my roommate in the room. I decided to sit in the courtyard and I was determined. But wait, God, if you want me here, I need You to let me know and I need to know right now. Two centimeters in, my angel appeared. She came to bring my school ID. Was this my sign? She told me that she needed to stay with me but she did not know why.

Grace. Alive.

Multiple "shes" came and went. I needed to control how they affected me. Rationalization became my primary source of sanity. It became my life—gracefully, not my lifestyle though. I could never deal with isolating myself based on my choices, nor did I feel that I was born that way. I was just enjoying life my own way.

After being graced to not commit homicide and suicide in the same night, I knew that I needed to change. I knew that I really needed to have a relationship with my Creator. I was addicted to drugs and alcohol, addicted to sex, suicidal, homicidal, and condemned to hell by most. But I was also loved and guided by Him who knew me before incarnation in my mother's womb. He told me that I was here for a purpose and no matter how I disrespected His design, He saw fit for me to continue with life.

I went back to church. I thought that I would find Him there. I quickly forgot that when I needed to reach out to Him, I found Him in the courtyard of my dorm. I went through the motions. I never completely healed though.

Suicide attempt number two proved that. After allowing a "him" to come back in, he shattered my heart and I saw no purpose to live. I will never forget it. I left national board review and called a friend that I trusted and told him that I needed him to pray. There was no way that I was going to carry forward if something didn't change. I cried, screamed, yelled, and wondered why this kept happening to me.

Graced. Alive.

A couple years later, doctors were convinced that I would never walk again. They just knew that I would never be able to breathe on my own. I went into heart failure five times in three days. I was diagnosed with a disease that only 7% of humans have ever survived.

Graced. Alive.

My hope was in humans. My life was dependent on my emotions. My life centered around my feelings. People did things to me. I fought against flesh and blood. Earth was my final resting place, so I needed to fight to control and preserve my reputation.

I openly share just a portion of my testimony to allow you to see that there is always hope. Understand that you inevitably control NOTHING! Control was the seed that I took from my first experience and I took that with me continually throughout my life until I finally healed. I was praying demons out of people and dealing with the same ones myself. I spoke in tongues and shouted like a pro without a true relationship with The Most High God. I had a relationship with the church and rituals.

I know that you have heard it before but I will say it again.... We are spiritual beings having a human experience. Circumstances are just that, circumstances. You have the choice in how you allow them to play out in your life. Being molested by a trusted person was a situation, not an excuse. It was a seed that I watered. I did not inspect my garden, I just watered what was there. That is what happens when we decide to allow the rituals of life to be our saving grace.

You are loved, forgiven, and free. The Most High God created you in infinite wisdom. There is great value in your life. There is purpose to fulfill. Once you know your purpose, you must be willing to give your all to the end for it. Anyone who has made a public mark on this world was willing to give it all for purpose. You will be scared. That happens. Face the fear and blow through it. You owe it to your purpose. This earth is not your final home. It is not until you let go of the fear of death that you will be willing to give your all for the sake of the greater. At that moment, you are completely aligned with your purpose.

Be free.

Forgiveness is essential. I had to forgive myself and I had to forgive the situation. If The Most High God saw fit to keep me alive, I had to honor that by living my life in the present. No longer could I allow the past to control my actions. The past was part of my foundation. That seed was no longer watered. Eventually it would starve itself out. I would never forget it, though. Although an amateur thing, I made a deal with God. I told Him that if I continued forward, I would do everything to be love to those who have trouble experiencing it. I told Him that another soul would not be love deprived at my expense.

Be on purpose.

Understand your vision, mission, and purpose. Once you do, give it your all. This is when you begin to live!

My mission of "loving humanity back to life through my hands, one beautiful soul at a time" comes from the inner workings of my soul. You will be used as you are. All of your circumstances have made you who you are now. What didn't kill you, didn't kill you!

Live a life that matters. Your vision, mission, and purpose are you. They can never be turned off. They evolve with time, but they are never separated from you, EVER. You live, eat, sleep, and breathe them at all times as you live as a Godly woman.

As a doctor, I have the responsibility of facilitating wellness in my clients. I choose to have an untraditional practice. Because of my understanding of spiritual warfare, I do not deal with physical symptoms as they are byproducts of spiritual battles that emotionally materialize into biochemical changes that manifest physically. I was there. Humans feed off of love. The key to wellness is understanding how to love humans. Yes, I do physical work but only at the request of the body's natural infinite wisdom.

As a human, I have the responsibility of loving humanity back to life whether they can afford my fees or not. I am responsible for feeding the hungry and clothing the naked. Every human, despite circumstance, is here on purpose. It is my human responsibility to help them understand that they are important and that they are responsible for their gift. Homelessness is a circumstance. Drug use is a circumstance. I was there. Depression is a circumstance. Again, I was there. Being in prison is a circumstance. NOTHING, and I mean nothing, is an excuse to allow any human to shine less than optimum. Understanding how the brain and spinal cord translates messages from The Most High God to the outside world is how chiropractic becomes my vehicle. I owe it to the world.

I love people back to life because life is dependent on love. I know why I am here.

Why are you here? Discover that and give it your all. That's how you live a Godly life as a human being, as a woman.

"Rejoicing in hope; patient in tribulation; continuing instant in prayer." – Romans 12:12

A lover of the sincerest nature, Dr. Crystal Jones uses chiropractic as her vehicle to love life back into humanity, one beautiful soul at a time. Her gifted hands led her to Los Angeles, Dallas, and throughout North Carolina, New York and Georgia for various inspirational speaking, teaching, and hands on chiropractic engagements. In 2014, she served at the National Track and Field Championships in Nassau, Bahamas, as the team chiropractor. She has also served in Ghana, Uganda, and soon, Canada. Dr. Jones values art, as she understands life, art, and love to be synonymous. In her spare time, she is a mentor, creator, writer, and editor. Her practice consists mostly of artists and athletes as she serves to facilitate the domino effect of excellence.

POWER
BY MORRISSA NICOLE

"For as he thinketh in his heart, so is he." Proverbs 23:7a

6 am. Snooze. 6:10 am. Snooze. 6:20 am. Turn off the alarm and I wait. I lie in bed slowly embracing this Tuesday morning. My day profession is a kindergarten educator, which means it is not just Tuesday, like so many others in the working world; it's Tuesday, Day 4 on the school's five-day cycle. It's my least favourite day of the cycle. For me, it means I have morning duty for 20 minutes in the bitter cold, greeting the children with a courageous warm smile to begin our day. I shiver at the thought of being outside. I am sure I share the sentiments of many when I say I hate the biting cold of winter. All the plans, ideas and thoughts that tucked me in the night before wake me up now and poke at me still unresolved. I glance at my clock, 6:45 am, it seems as though time and I are in a cross country race and I am trailing far behind. I have decided already today is not my day. I arise and finally decide it's time to pick up some speed in this race. Immediately, I fall into my morning routine moving as swiftly as I can. I whisper a prayer of gratitude to God, thanking Him for keeping me, asking Him for grace, patience, wisdom, and protection for myself and my family, and rush to start a day that has already begun without me.

I jump into a car that refuses to start. Already, I feel as though this day is pivoted against me. Angered, I pull my key out, push it back into the ignition and try again, with only the fifth time leading to success. I know this early morning battle is going to make me late for work. I sigh knowing that there is no rewind button to this day. I remember my prayer this morning and that seems to bring a bit of peace. I shift into drive and speed down the roadways. Just as I am about to switch lanes, I get cut off by another driver who speeds up probably in a hurry much like myself. However, that doesn't stop me from blowing my horn and throwing up my hands. I grind my teeth; this is not going to be a good day!

Quickly, I scurry across the parking lot dropping my purse and its entire contents onto the snow-covered ground. Everything is wet including my iPhone and iPad. Gathering everything into my arms, I rush into the school frantically yelling at winter to go away! With my luck, it may actually just hear me and do exactly as I ask. I feel like this is a really bad sports game, like a soccer game. If I had a commentator in this game, I would imagine him saying *"Tuesday vs. Morrissa! Well folks, it doesn't seem like she's ever going to make headway in this game. This girl's fighting a losing battle. Better luck tomorrow."*

Better luck tomorrow is right! If I happen to stumble on a magic lamp like Aladdin on my way to work, one of my three wishes would be skipping this day. Of course, this is not Disney; this is the real world.

Getting into the classroom, I dry off my purse and electronics and grab my lukewarm coffee sitting on my counter given to me by a wonderful co-teacher. I start with my duty in the kindergarten yard. The bell rings and the children flood the yard. One by one they kiss their parents goodbye running to embrace me with their tiny hands wrapped around my legs. "Hi!" they shout with excitement, squeezing my legs. I smile. Despite the cold, the tiniest little bear hug leaves me warm and happy. The bell rings and the children all shuffle in a blob-like formation into the school. As I am just about to close the school door, a child yells, "Wait for me!" and slides in just in time. We will call this child Jack. Jack often needs many reminders about the day's rules and routines and often needs several time outs for the day. With patience, I smile and say, "Come on in, Jack," and close the door behind me wishing for an easier rest of the day.

How quickly did that wish vanish, when the door closed and my fingers were crushed! In a painful panic I dropped my coffee showering myself in caffeine from my jacket down to my boots. I hear the commentator say, *"Tuesday 5, Morrissa 0."* Just great! The kids think it's funny, some stare in shock and others continue into the class as noticing nothing. I manage to force a smile as I enter the class with my throbbing hand dripping coffee.

Then Jack begins. This morning, he is having a hard time settling in. I was already frustrated by my own morning battle and now adding Jack to the mix just might make it worse. He is absolutely refusing to listen. Instead of taking his winter clothes off, he wanders into the play area. After several reminders to take his clothes off, Jack goes on his first time out for the day. I tried, I thought. I really tried. I thought I had the patience but right now my patience is at 25% and that's not much in a kindergarten classroom. Jack then decides it would be fun to smack a child across the face with his snow pants. He proceeds to his second time out. I sigh. I am beginning to hate this day. I look at the clock it reads 9:15 am and I feel like I am losing! *"Tuesday 7, Morrissa 0! Where is the defense?" says my imaginary commentator.*

He is right! Where is the defense? Where is the peace that I need to make it through this day? Where is God to provide a quiet, still voice to the ever-raging waters since 6 am this morning? Didn't I pray this morning? Didn't I dedicate this day to the Lord? I specifically remember asking for patience, wisdom, and grace! This is the day that the Lord has made. I will rejoice and be glad in it. Rejoice!? I can't even think on that scripture right now! I am too flustered and angry to even think about rejoicing. This is a day where I felt everything had gone wrong! The smallest things were adding up. I can feel myself losing my cool!

Let's tally it up, shall we? First, I woke up realizing it was a Day 4 on my school schedule which I already expressed was my least favourite day. Then, I remembered it was winter and I hate being in the cold, not to mention I have cold uticaria (a skin allergic reaction to cold) which doesn't help at all. Next, my car wouldn't start, making me late. I get cut off on the road nearly causing an accident before work! Both my iPhone and iPad are still soaking wet from my dropping them along with everything else in my purse in the snow. I crush my fingers in the door and spill coffee all over me becoming an early morning comedian for my kindergarteners. Finally, Jack comes in misbehaving and defiant.

As a woman, I do not feel very graceful. I do not feel I can handle any more of this with tact or patience. As a Christian woman, I feel even worse. I shouldn't feel this way. I feel guilty for feeling this way. And now I am angry about feeling guilty about feeling this way! I am a Christian, I should be at peace and should be floating through the day as a butterfly. But instead, I feel like pulling my hair out, beating my chest, and yelling whatever comes to my mouth.

Jack is still on time out. I look at him. What am I going to say to encourage him to feel better about his day? I calmly walk over, grab a chair, and looks down. My heart drops because I know that he realizes he made some poor choices to start his day.

"Jack," I start as I try to figure out what I'm going to say next. "You have made some pretty not so good choices." I list off all the poor choices he made that put him on time out. "Why do you think you did those things?" I asked him, genuinely wanting to know. He shrugs and shuffles his feet on the floor still looking down.

"Look at me, Jack." I wait until his eyes meet mine. I smile. "You are a great boy. You have chosen to do some not so great things, and that's ok because everyone makes mistakes. But doing it over and over again has consequences. Doing things good or bad have consequences. Do you know what that means?"

He nods.

"In this case, your consequence for not listening many times put you on time out which I can see by your face makes you very sad," I said. I stop and I wait. I have no idea where to go next with this conversation. He looks down again. I feel for him because even though he was defiant and hurting his peers, he is still very young and this simple mistake does not define him. Suddenly, my heart melts and I want to restart his day and make him feel better. I look at the clock and it's 9:30 am. I start again, "Listen, the day is not over there is still a lot of the day left."

I hold out my arms really wide to show him and exaggerate how much time we had left in the school day. "Look at this time you have left today. That's a lot. It's bigger than my arms can stretch!"

He gives me a sideways smile. I can tell I am getting through to him. "Listen Jack, you have the power to make this day a better day. You make the choices. You do! You have the power to turn this day around by making good choices. I believe that you have the power to do it. I know you have the power to do it. Do you believe that you have the power?" He nods with a big grin on his face. "Then go and do it!" He gives me a high five and he runs to the play area. I walk away feeling better. I don't know why but I felt better. Then it dawned on me. As crazy as this day had been for me I had the power to change it and make it better! It's only 9:30 am and I still have a lot of the day left. Besides, isn't that what I told Jack and didn't I expect him to do exactly what I said... using his power to change the day? How could I tell him to do it if I first didn't try it myself?

I, Morrissa, have the power to change this day. This will be a good day! In fact, one of my first mistakes this morning was already admitting defeat. At 6:45 this morning I had already made the choice that this would not be a good day. I walked with that attitude and carried it on my shoulders like a knapsack of Christmas toys. I tied it around my foot like a ball and chain, even wore it around my waist like a belt! Who am I to determine that a day that the Lord has made with brand new mercies and an opportunity at life would be my worst day? I decided the fate of the day before I really awoke and with each step I took, I confirmed it. I spoke it aloud and I believed it would be exactly what I called it out to be, a bad day. I had the power to choose what day I wanted and willingly and openly accepted a bad day. Now I am not saying that the things that happened above could have been completely avoided. But maybe Day 4s are the children's favourite day of the school cycle because they love that my face is the first face they see in the morning. Maybe my car didn't start because it was keeping me from an accident I missed because I was 5-10 minutes behind time. Maybe if I wasn't rushing and I just walked I wouldn't have dropped all my personal items in the snow. I could go on with the list of maybes and maybe nots and there will always be some uncertainty there. But one thing was certain - I had and always have the power over every single day. I was choosing, much like Jack, to make this a better day. I think my commentator would now say, *"That's it. She's finally gotten the hang of it! Ladies and gentleman, she is in the groove! Don't stop her now. She is on a roll!"*

It was 2:45 pm and the school day was coming to a close. Children were tidying the class and getting ready to go home and tell their parents all about their day. I stood at the coat rack monitoring some children getting ready with bursts of giggles and excitement escaping the cubby area. There were children eagerly putting their snow pants on and even some children putting them on backwards. All in all, it was a good day. Suddenly, I felt tiny little fingers wrap around my hand and pull ever so slightly, just enough to get my attention. I turned. It was Jack. "Ms. Brown," he said as he beamed up at me, "I have the power! I had a good day!" I crouched down so we were face to face and exclaimed, "You had a fantastic day! You always have the power!" He replied by showing me all his teeth in the biggest smile I had ever seen. Then he ran off to get ready. *"Morrissa 10, Tuesday 7."* I won the game.

I want to let you know that I didn't speak to that boy once after our morning conversation, I had even forgot about him.

There is a scripture in Prov. 18:21 that says, *"Death and life are in the power of the tongue."* It is the power of positive thinking and of positive speaking. It is literally written everywhere in the Bible! If we applied it daily, how happy would we be? I am sure that you can go through this story and pick out everywhere I went wrong. Yes, I prayed and started my morning off right, but I had no faith in my prayer. How quickly can we fall into recitation, especially when our mornings move so fast? As the day progressed and things happened, I was so quick to question God before questioning and analyzing myself. The next time you face a difficult situation in life, I want you to know that just like 5-year-old Jack, you have the power to turn any situation right side up. You have the power. I have the power. We have the power.

Morrissa Nicole is a vibrant young woman for Christ. She accepted the Lord at the age of 5 and has been an ambassador for Christ since. Morrissa serves as a youth pastor at The Worship Center. At 23, she was ordained as a minister. Her passion for the community is shown in her work with the city program Y.E.S. Community Group to inspire youth. Morrissa is also an international recording artist who recently released her self-titled album. When she isn't working on her music, she can be seen acting in live theatre and on television.

BECOMING A GODLY WOMAN
BY SHINEKA KARIM

Deciding on whether someone is a Godly woman or not usually takes the form of a small checklist. Our faith and relationship with Christ have been minimized to a checklist of do's and don'ts based on what others before us have done. As women of God, we often look to pattern ourselves after women we admire in the gospel. Then, if we think we need to, we reference the real source, the Word of God. The checklist usually looks something like this, especially for young single women:
1. Have you accepted Jesus Christ as your Lord and Savior?
2. Are you willing to serve in the church?
3. Are you trying to live a life of purity?
4. Do you pray?

Congratulations! You are now looked at as a Godly woman. The sad part is that since many churches are not getting back to the basics of creating disciples, we are being left to figuring out the standards of holiness. That is part of the reason many do not understand that holiness is *still* right. The conditions or standards of being a Godly woman should not change as the calendar year changes. Being a Godly woman is based on the Word of God and since the Word of God transcends time, the standards of being a Godly woman should be able to stand the test of time. Godly women are women who show consistency in all areas of their lives. Will we make mistakes? Yes! Will we reach moments of uncertainty? Absolutely! Will we feel uncomfortable going against the grain and flow of society? Definitely!

As Godly women, the main thing we must understand is that being Godly starts and ends with discipline. We must have discipline in our relationship with God. If we don't, we will have difficulty in other areas of our lives. Discipline is defined as an activity, exercise, or a regimen that develops or improves a skill; training. When we discipline ourselves, we create a regimen towards a goal. Just like when deciding to get in shape, we make a goal and then put a plan in place. We can view the act of discipline in our spiritual life the same way. A disciplined relationship with Christ involves an active prayer life, devotion to Him, studying His word, a daily submission to His will, and a dedicated life of worship.

When I talk about an active prayer life, I mean do you know the components of prayer? Do you study scriptures so that you pray effectively? Are your prayers limited to the things that you want in your life? Are your prayers selfish or rooted in God's will? Are you praying daily, multiple times during the day? If we believe that prayer is powerful then we must be disciplined in our prayer life. We must make active decisions to learn about prayer. We must get in the habit of actually praying when asked to pray. We must learn God's language by studying his Word. This allows us to not only speak and petition during prayer, but also to listen. Prayer is a relationship that is developed day by day. It leads us into a devotion to God.

What is devotion to God?

Devotion involves yielding our hearts to Him. It involves developing an unconditional love for the One that paid the ultimate price for our lives. The secret to devotion is love. We cannot simply love Him as we have loved passed boyfriends or even family members. Our love for Him must surpass any love that we have ever felt. It is a love that cannot always be put into words, but can truly be felt. Our love for Christ creates a devotion to do His will, to trust Him in all things, and to never be ashamed of him. Devotion creates a desire to develop and grow. It causes us to want to be pruned and molded so that we begin to look more like the One we love and less like the world.

Even as I type this, I know that many of us rarely make a connection with the difference, but I will ask the question anyway. Are we studying or merely reading the Word of God? I know we get up and we may read a devotional or a scripture to start our day, but do we really study. It is very rare that we apply the concept of studying the Bible in the same way that we study for a course in school. We map out time. We structure our schedules around study time so that we can prepare for big tests or exams, but the test of life comes regularly and we do not study so that we can prepare. As a result, we are shocked when things come up and we do not know how to handle them. We often say that we do not have the time and even if we do not verbalize it, our actions speak for us. Our actions say that other things take priority in our lives. Hearing my sisters say that they do not read the Bible because they do not understand, makes me want to remind them that we are supposed to study it instead of just read it. When we study, we learn God's voice. When we study, we understand how the Word applies in every aspect of our lives. When we study, we learn to view it as a manual for life and without it we are headed to an unknown destination without a GPS.

The 'S' Word

It is one of the things that I am working on the most. I think submission is hard for all of us, including men. Submission has received such a bad reputation that Christians are not getting the real understanding of what it means. Submission is an absolute necessity. Without submission, we cannot completely function as Godly women. If we cannot submit fully to Christ, we do not understand how to submit to leadership and that creates havoc in our households. Submission is rarely talked about in the church, but often addressed in the world. To submit means to come under the mission. What is the mission you ask? Our mission as Godly women is to:

- Live a life that brings God glory in all aspects.
- Carry out God's plan for our lives.
- Share the gospel in a variety of ways.
- Function and carry ourselves as daughters of a King.

How can we do these things if we are acting in disobedience and unwilling to submit for fear of appearing weak? The world has created a fear in women, one that comes from not being in charge, of being subservient, and of being viewed as a weaker vessel. This fear is being instilled alongside the Bible and trust me the Bible is not winning.

My sisters, we have to take a step back and really understand the purpose of submission and how beneficial it is in our walk with Christ. The best example of a submitted life in my opinion is Christ who was fully submitted to God's will and plan for Him. Christ was still able to do amazing things. He still had a purpose. The act of submission is allowing God's will to supersede ours. It is verbally saying and believing what Mary said when she found out she would be with child: "Be it unto me according to thy word." Submission does not mean that we as women are less important. Submission does not mean that we do not have a role in the Kingdom of God. Submission does not mean that we will be walked over even overlooked. It means that we value and respect the plans that God has for our lives and the lives that are connected to our obedience. It means that we understand fully that obedience is better than sacrifice. Sisters, I encourage you just as I have to encourage myself to submit daily. A submitted life is a life of freedom not bondage!

Sisters, I write this to you to provide wisdom and not to bring forth any harsh speech. I pray that you take these principles that I am sharing to heart. We have to actively seek wisdom. We have to demand in a sense that we are taught the basics based on the Word. Instead of allowing disobedience to be passed down from generation to generation, we truly need to pass down knowledge of godliness. Godliness is not about perfection. I am nowhere near perfect. Godliness is about being persistent in getting it right. It is about admitting when we are wrong and working to correct the behavior. It is about giving our best each day. Godliness is not about wearing a title as a badge of honor. As Christian women, we do not need anything else that makes us look pretentious. Godly women are humble in heart. They do not need to prove to others that they are Godly. The goal is to keep striving and not to ever think we have arrived. I encourage you to continue in your pursuit. To let your life be an example to others, not because of the recognition, but because we are supposed to share our light with others.

We cannot allow society to dictate what godliness means. We cannot allow society to tell us that we must change our standards to that we can be more accepted by others. Everything that we need in order to understand how to handle the changes that happen in the world around us in the Bible. A queen does not take off her crown so that it makes others more comfortable when they are addressing her. She carries herself as royalty and you should do the same. We are to be caring of others, but that does not mean completely negate the standard that is on our lives. It is not always going to be easy or something that we want to do or something that we understand, especially when the reaction from others is not pleasant. But we press anyway just as Jesus did in the Garden of Gethsemane.

Sisters, I pour out my heart to you because as a 30-year-old woman I can honestly say that I do not recall anyone sharing these things with me. We accept Jesus Christ as our Lord and Savior and sadly, we are left alone, at times, to muddle the waters of our faith. We get a good word on Sundays and we may even go to Bible study, but that usually ends up being a mini sermon. In many instances, the basics of godliness have gotten lost in the shuffle of gaining members. So I encourage you to pursue godliness on your own. Make it an area of focus. Reach out to other sisters because we have to support one another and understand that we are not meant to do this on our own. There will be moments that make you just want to run away from your faith, but if you have a support system of sisters in place that understands what you are dealing with, it makes it a little easier to handle life. There will be moments where you are not sure if you have made the right decision to trust God and to live your life in a way that is always pleasing to Him. Sometimes you will fall down. But the beauty is in being able to get back up. The pathway towards godliness is a daily journey. It is a decision to be in tune with what God wants for your life. It is a decision to tune out the noise and confusion of the world while leaning on His everlasting arms.

Shineka Karim is a wife and mother that has a desire to spread God's word around the world through books, coaching, and speaking. The Atlanta native is extremely passionate about impacting the lives of others, especially women, by encouraging them to live their best life now! She can be reached at www.shinekakarim.com.

HE HAS A MASTER PLAN
BY JANELLE NUNES

I had to try my best to hold back my tears as the children sang "He's a miracle-working God" with such joy and anticipation. Some even danced and played tambourines. These children knew how to make a joyful noise unto the Lord despite many of them being barefoot, wearing clothes that didn't fit, and having eaten nothing but cornmeal morning, noon, and night for as long as they could remember. There I stood in the dusty make-shift classroom in the mountains of Swaziland, blessed by the children's exuberance and grateful to the Lord for such a wonderful opportunity. While I had always wanted to go on missions and had always been interested in connecting with people of different cultures, I never imagined that such an opportunity would arise. I was shy, fearful, struggling with dizziness, and my community was quite homogenous but the Lord has a way of taking us from where we are to where we need to be in order to fulfill His plan for our lives.

Shaky headaches. That's what I used to call them. Eventually, I started to refer to these disruptions to my daily routines as dizzy spells. Regardless of what they were called, they frustrated me to no avail. One minute I was doing perfectly fine, the next I was desperately holding on to someone or something waiting for the shakiness to end. At times, when there was nothing to hold on to, I would just sit on the ground and wait for the feeling to pass. Sometimes I would crawl towards a comfortable safe spot. As a child, it was upsetting but manageable, especially since my parents could easily scoop me off the ground and place me somewhere cozy to rest until I recovered. As I grew older, it became more difficult.

What teenager wants to be known for being the one who crawls on the floor in the high school hallway because it is too difficult for her to stand? Who wants to be known as the student who vomits in the office when her dizziness causes nausea? That's definitely not the kind of attention that I wanted. Thankfully, my identity as a student was not solely based my health. The Lord allowed me to be a strong student academically and provided me with opportunities to work in the school library, participate actively in the school music department, and run for several years on the track and field team. Nevertheless, the office secretaries still knew me a little too well for my episodes of being unable to walk in a straight line.

I was a regular at the doctor's office and had become quite accustomed to my name being among the prayer requests at prayer services. The doctors had no idea what was causing the problem and God remained silent. I must admit that there were times I believed that I had some kind of unknown disease that would be discovered upon my death. I delayed learning to drive for fear of the consequences of dizziness behind the wheel. I was quite satisfied taking the bus and doing everything locally for the sake of safety. Even with post-secondary education opportunities waiting, I decided to play it safe and applied to two local universities: York University and University of Toronto. Since we were required to apply to a minimum of three post-secondary institutions, I also applied to Queen's University on a whim… or so I thought.

God has a way of redirecting our lives. I received letters of acceptance and scholarships to both York and U of T. After much thought, I decided that I would go to York since they were offering a full scholarship. I completed the paperwork and headed to the mailbox. Before mailing the envelope, I collected the mail first. I gasped when I saw a large enveloped addressed to me from Queen's University. I closed the mailbox and ran back home, completely forgetting to mail the letter to York. God would have it that I was accepted into the concurrent education program at Queen's. For some reason, it just felt right. While I had not intended on going away to school, I knew that this was part of God's plan for my life.

I was excited and nervous to begin this new chapter in my life. I loved school and I loved learning but I knew it would be hard to leave my family and all of the familiar components of my life in the GTA. I was also worried about how I would manage on my own with the dizziness that seemed to plague my life. Even so, I knew that I couldn't spend my entire life living in fear. As though to reassure me, the Lord allowed something miraculous to happen during the summer before my first year away from home.

I had participated in a special partnership with the Bank of Montreal during my final year of high school and had managed to acquire a summer job in one of the main offices downtown as a result. Every day, I took the GO train to Union Station and then either walked several blocks to work or took the subway, depending on how I was feeling. That summer, I had another bout of dizziness and stayed home from work for several days. When I returned to work, I hopped on the GO train as usual that morning and then decided to take the subway instead of walking to the office. I walked through the busy GO train station and crossed over to the side where I could take the subway. Since it was rush hour, there were people everywhere. It was almost overwhelming. Actually, it *was* overwhelming. As I tried to head over to the escalator to go underground towards the train, the dizziness returned... with a vengeance. I did not know what to do. I thought: "Lord, why now?"

The dizziness wouldn't go away and it was becoming more and more difficult to walk straight and maintain my vision. I felt like I was going to fall down. All I could do was grab on to the nearest person to gain some stability. I was surprised to hear a familiar voice speaking to me as the individual guided me towards a bench to sit down. It was my cousin. I had never bumped into him downtown prior to that day (or the several summers after that encounter). It had to be God and it was then that I knew that everything was going to be ok. God had chosen not to heal me of my ailment but He showed me that He was still with me. The dizziness provided me with countless testimonies and reminded me of God's faithfulness and tender loving care. It was only fitting that during my last Sunday service at church before going away to school, a minister sang a song that lingered in my heart throughout the years that I spent living in Kingston, Ontario:

>I trust in God wherever I may be,
>Upon the land, or on the rolling sea,
>For come what may, from day to day,
>My heav'nly Father watches over me.
>
>I trust in God, I know He cares for me;
>On mountain bleak or on the stormy sea;
>Though billows roll, He keeps my soul;
>My heav'nly Father watches over me.
>
>He makes the rose an object of His care,
>He guides the eagle through the pathless air,
>And surely He remembers me;
>My heav'nly Father watches over me.
>
>William C. Martin

My Heavenly Father surely did watch over me in Kingston and He groomed me while I was there as well. First, I had to learn to fully rely on Him. The dizziness did not stop while I was living away from home. I still had moments when I struggled to even get the toothpaste onto my toothbrush, but I just learned to be even more prayerful in everything that I did, including when a bill arrived that I didn't have the money to pay (and didn't want to burden my parents by asking for money). I just laid it before the Lord. Sure enough, a cheque came in the mail from the university for the exact amount. When I called to inquire about why the cheque was sent, no one was able to give an answer. Everyone to whom I was transferred on the telephone during the query simply said, "I don't know where the money came from but the money is yours, your name is on the cheque." All I could say was: "Thank you, Lord!"

While I had moved to Kingston for the purpose of schooling, my learning did not only occur in the classroom. Within the first few days, I had flipped through the phonebook to find a church to attend. (Yes, there was a time before smartphones and the Internet that we looked for information in the telephone book). I made a call and was greeted by a lovely lady on the other end of the phone. The woman turned out to be the pastor's wife and she was just as lovely in person as she was on the telephone. My new pastor and his wife loved me as though I were family and my time with them was a valuable and important growing experience especially since I was the only Black member of an all-white congregation.

All my life I had been a member of an all-black, predominantly Jamaican congregation. The culture heavily influenced our worship, our fellowship activities, and our interactions. I had often questioned this phenomenon thinking that if Jesus died on the cross for everyone, and we lived in such a multicultural society, why on earth was our congregation so homogenous? Perhaps it was more troubling to me because I was Canadian and my world outside of church had always been diverse. I often wondered what it would be like for an individual of a different culture to join our congregation and I also craved opportunities to fellowship with believers of different backgrounds.

Although the change of environment caused a bit of culture shock - the music, traditions and food were different - it also helped to broaden my vision and ignite my passions. The services seemed shorter but we met more frequently for worship, Bible study, youth activities, and small group fellowship in one another's homes. And we prayed a whole lot for each other and the community. The emphasis was always on growing in relationship with God and reaching out so that others could do the same. Jesus was always at the very centre of everything that we did. There was no hierarchy and no hype. It was never about how well anyone sang, how well someone dressed up, or how eloquently someone spoke. Everything was about Jesus. I was reminded to look past culture, even church culture, and focus on Jesus and share Him with others.

The pastor often told us about how his parents were missionaries in Pakistan and that, as a result, he grew up surrounded by a completely different culture. Within my community, the term "missionary" had been used as a term of endearment and respect for the older women in the church. I'm not sure how that came to be but that was the reality that I had experienced for most of my life. It was neat to hear about these other kinds of "missionaries". I could hardly wait for Missions Sundays because we gave a special offering towards both home and local missions and would take extra time to pray for those who were serving as missionaries. We often had special visits from missionaries who were ministering in other parts of the world. I loved to listen to them as they shared their experiences, their passion, and their prayer requests. I always wrote a list in my prayer journal so I would remember to pray for the needs that they expressed. Those Sundays were a treat for me and I was always excited to call my mother and tell her about the missionaries who came to visit. I had no idea that one day I, too, would be able to tell stories about standing beside an interpreter as I shared the Word of God and taught others about the Lord.

While I absolutely loved living in Kingston, the time came for me to return home. I was able to secure a permanent teaching position with the local school board and I returned to the routine of working in a diverse community from Monday to Friday and then serving God as a member of my homogenous church congregation on weeknights and weekends. After a while, my excitement about missions seemed to fade to the background as I focused on preparing lesson plans, marking papers, attending choir rehearsals, and teaching Sunday school lessons. Still, I couldn't help but emphasize to my Sunday school students that Jesus died for everyone regardless of their culture. I also began meeting regularly with some of my teacher colleagues to pray for our administrators, colleagues, and students. The prayer needs became more important than our different cultures and denominational backgrounds. We needed Jesus at the centre of our school and our classrooms, period.

I thoroughly enjoyed working with my students and was so glad to have met such a wonderful network of colleagues with whom I could practice my faith in a secular environment. Everything seemed to be coming together and I figured that I had fallen into God's rhythm for my life. While the health challenges had not subsided, the Lord continued to be my keeper and I was beginning to appreciate the testimonies that I was able to share as a result. When the opportunity came for me to travel to Swaziland to teach children about Jesus, my heart was overflowing. I thought, Lord, you prepared me by teaching me to trust you with my health, allowing me to interact with mission-minded people, strengthening my prayer life, and then placing me in a classroom where I could grow as a teacher. Although the idea of going to an unknown country with people that I had never met (other than one other sister from my church) seemed very scary, I felt ready.

We were heading into a rural area of Swaziland to spend a couple of weeks at an orphanage and serve the community. The life expectancy in Swaziland at the time was 32 years due to the AIDS epidemic. Our mission team did a lot of preparation ahead of time. We fundraised, collected donations, and spent a lot of time in prayer. Our team was subdivided into groups: some would build additional housing, some would work in the kitchen, some would teach basic skills (i.e. sewing, building benches), some would prepare sports activities for the kids, and some would teach Bible classes. I was a part of the team that taught Bible classes to the children. I had to learn to simplify what I was saying so that my eleven-year-old interpreter would be able to translate for me.

It turned out that the children living on the orphanage were way better off than the children living in the rural community. Organizations send donations to orphanages, but do not send donations to random huts in rural communities. Word spread that we were at the orphanage and children from the community walked miles to join us. While many of them enjoyed the activities and the Bible stories, I suspect that many of them came mostly for the meal and for the items that we were able to send home with them. We had shipped the donations that we had collected a few months ahead of time and were able to sort out the materials and distribute them to members of the community. Some of the children received shoes for the first time and others were glad to trade in their old tattered clothes for new clothes. We provided clothing, shoes, and personal hygiene items for the adults in the community along with medical supplies for the local clinic. We were also blessed to set up a library with books and computers that had been donated by a company in Canada.

The children at the orphanage held their own devotions before dinner every day. Although this was done in their own language, they often invited a few of us to join them. One of the older children would read from the Bible, share an exhortation, and then open the floor for the other children to share. Sometimes the children would share a song, or a testimony, and sometimes they would confess something that they had done and ask the rest of the children to pray for them. Then, they would sing ever so beautifully and say a prayer of thanksgiving for the food that they were about to receive. Every meal was the same.... cornmeal that they had helped to prepare by taking the kernels off the maize and grinding them before sending them to the kitchen to be washed and cooked. These children were an inspiration.

The mission team met at the beginning and the end of every day to worship, read the Bible, and pray. We often began each session by singing these lyrics written by Paul Baloche & Glenn Packiam: "As morning dawns and evening fades, You inspire songs of praise that rise from earth to touch Your heart and glorify Your Name." It was a great way to begin and end each day. Many of us stayed up late to journal, to talk about the Lord, and to talk about the future. I really enjoyed our time of fellowship. One night in particular stands out in my mind. After dinner, we decided to take our flashlights and have devotion outside. I will never forget standing on the mountain, looking over into the horizon under the stars and singing, "Oh Lord my God, when I in awesome wonder consider all the world Thy hand has made..." By the time we got to "How Great Thou Art", the tears came streaming down my face. I still think of that moment every time I sing that hymn.

My time in Swaziland changed my life. It also prepared me for ministry opportunities in Indonesia and Malaysia two years later. By the time I landed in Indonesia, I was able to speak to a large crowd of adults and young people about God's faithfulness. With the help of an interpreter, I shared my personal testimony of how I had struggled with my health and had made many visits to the hospital during the months leading up to the trip. As I spoke, I realized that the frustration that I had gone through during that time provided me with a testimony that would change someone else's life. I was able to be a witness of the healing and sustaining power of God. Just as the Lord had brought me through a long process to prepare me to travel to Swaziland, He had placed challenges in my life to give me a message to share in Indonesia. When God is working in our lives, we may not always be privy to the big picture but we must always trust that He has a Master Plan.

Janelle enjoys pouring into the lives of others and considers herself blessed to have the opportunity to do so on a daily basis through her career as an educator. Janelle also enjoys expressing herself through music. In addition to singing, she currently plays the clarinet with a Christian orchestra during her spare time.

SISTERS IN PRAISE

MEETING THE MASTER
BY SARAH N.J. ANDERSON

"So it's been kind of a long road, but it was a good journey altogether."
Sidney Poitier

Life Verse: Romans 8:28
My name is Sarah Naomi Jennifer Anderson. Born August 22nd 1989 and I am the modern day "woman with the issue". I am on a journey to become whole and this is my story...

I am the middle child of three kids and the second daughter born to Dr. Denroy Washington Anderson and Ms. Yvette Anderson. Growing up we lived in the east end of the city in the Rouge Valley area in a suburban town house. My father is an engineer and an ordained pastor so I grew up in a comfortable, yet strict Christian household where the fear of the Lord was instilled in our minds and lives at an early age.

I remember on Saturday evenings my sister and I would sit between my mother's knees crying about having to get our hair washed and combed in time for Sunday service. Our clothes would be ironed (skirts of course), stockings laid out and everything prepared so that the morning would go smoothly. It was routine. In my formative years, we attended a church called New Life Tabernacle in the east end of the city. I was born and raised on the pew of this large Holy Ghost-filled

Pentecostal church that was pastored by Hazel Catudella, a dynamic and powerful woman of God. I love and honor that woman and vow to carry out her legacy of strong prayer, ministry, faith, praise and worship until God calls me home. Pastor, I love you!

Both of my parents were very active in the church so there was a no nonsense policy in our home. For those of us who know what it's like having parents who are in ministry, it can be a blessing and a curse. (I'll explain more about that later).

Before my brother was born, my sister and I were involved in everything! And by everything, I mean absolutely everything – the youth choir, adult choir, Sunday school, youth group, Saturday morning prayer, mid-week service... you name it, we were there!

At 5, I remember learning how to recite and to pray the scriptures. As an adult woman, I thank God for those times with my father because I didn't realize how much I was retaining for when I really needed those words later in life. The Lord sees our end from our beginning and knew that a season when my back would be against the wall and I wouldn't have the time or strength to search the book for them. I am so thankful that he made a way to ensure that the word was already hidden in my heart. The good thing about being raised by Christian parents and being actively involved in a solid church body is that you learn a lot. You have deacons, elders, church mothers, God-parents, aunts and uncles who are always on you about "holy living" or looking like you're living holy. But in that environment, you also miss out on a lot.

Those same people that I honor and bless God for because they played a huge role in helping to shape and develop me into the woman I am today, also had a way of omitting parts of their stories and testimonies that could have helped the next generation. There were a lot of rules but no one could tell me why those rules existed. I am an inquisitive person by nature so if you say, "Sarah, don't do that!" I need to know why. Until you can tell me why I shouldn't do something, 99.9% of the time I will do it.

When time came for me to grow into my own and to face life as a young person, I realized that I wasn't as prepared as I thought. I had so many unanswered questions and was walking around with so much doubt and fear. These people that I looked up to and that I trusted spiritually thought all was well with me because: I was Pastor Anderson's daughter; I could stand in front of the church sing a few hymns or exhort, the power would fall, and God would move; and I did it all in my long skirt. But the church family didn't see that inside was a very confused young lady. But being raised in the church, I knew how to do all of it very well. So everything was okay... or was it?

We left that church when I was 10 and we began attending a new church further east. By 15, I had learned how to fake my way through a service and conduct a youth meeting. At the same time, I was screaming on the inside, begging for someone to save me from myself. At our new church, I met some lifelong friends who were older and some I thought were more seasoned believers than I and who could possibly help me navigate through these crazy developmental years. I connected with a few big brothers and sisters that I consider family and I am still in contact with them. Some of those relationships were not healthy or beneficial to me and some were downright abusive and added nothing but more fuel to my already raging internal fire.

Some of them were Godsends. They helped me dig through and tear down some of the religious walls that had been erected in my mind and heart. I thank God for their contribution to my life and ministry.

From 15-17, I spent a lot of time being discipled in the things of God. Despite the fact that I was still considerably young, I was struggling with my identity and knowing my place in this "Kingdom" that I kept hearing about. The church ensured me that I was still very much involved in ministry. But even while serving, I still felt something was missing. It's interesting to be among so many people and still feel so lost, broken, and alone. I knew that there had to be more to this walk of faith than coming to a service and going home feeling just as drained as when I got there. There was a deep longing and thirsting for something more than what a Sunday, Wednesday or Friday night service could quench.

Through age 21, my story took a turn for the worst. My religious upbringing and coaching was put to the test and I failed. I realized that I couldn't keep me. The longing, the emptiness and the desire to feel full was so overwhelming that I started rebelling, smoking, drinking, and engaging in promiscuous behavior.

I attended as many clubs that I could. I loved the nightlife and loved to party. The music, the weed, and the drinks put me in a place where only what I wanted mattered. The more I drank and smoked, the more that emptiness was filled. During this same time, I still attended conference after conference, praying meeting after prayer meeting, youth event after youth event, with people who were just as confused.

The keeping power of God is amazing to me. Surprisingly, my high school sweetheart and I remained virgins, despite being together from sixth grade until my last year in high school. I was very serious about keeping myself until I met the one God kept for me... until about the age of 18 when I met "him". I entered into a relationship with this young man who appeared to be everything I wanted. I mean, this dude was it! Tall, dark-skinned, in church, handsome, athletic, and with a beautiful killer smile (just like Daddy's!) that could light up any room. And to top it off, he had a smooth deep voice. Like... whoa! A young "man of God." At this point, God started open heart surgery on your girl!

In my head, we were going be that young Godly couple that would change the world.

Instead of seeking more of God, we were having sex while still coming to church on a Sunday morning and singing on the praise team and with the choir. It became a regular thing. I knew early on in the relationship that it was wrong but I also thought double standard was how life as a young "Christian" was supposed to be! No one really told us why we should stop. At a young age, I came to the belief that it was ok to proclaim you're a Christian and live an opposing lifestyle during the week. Now that I'm grown and have a clearer understanding of what being a woman of God means, I laugh at my immature thinking. I understand fully that the grace of God is not to be taken for granted and that there is a standard of living required for us to uphold.

Like many of us, after living a double life, a decision had to be made. Unfortunately, I gave in and fell victim to lust. During this highly sexual relationship, I became addicted to sex. It was this insatiable desire that I thought would never be fulfilled. Being bound by masturbation, pornography and perversions is common when you align yourself with someone who only speaks to and feeds your flesh.

While fighting through this whirlwind of emotions, conviction, and confusion, God called me to the ministry. He spoke clearly and specifically to me about what he created me to do. In the middle of one of the biggest storms of my life, the Master of the sea heard my muffled cry. It made no sense to me, at that time, that He would call me to lead nations of young women back to Him. But I understood that God sees our end from our beginning.

Unfortunately, I continued to be intimate with this young man and I got deeper and deeper into the dark side of sexual sin. I still had the need to feel desired and loved so I tried to stick it out. I thought that my love for him and to him would change him but I quickly realized that love doesn't work that way. I felt crazy, spiritually schizophrenic. Every day, I woke up feeling like my world was spinning and spiraling out of control. I had trouble discerning between truth and lies. It was hard for me to recognize real from fake, I was unable to think clearly, and my perception and ability to reason were clouded. I was still attending church and trying to keep a game face but I was losing my mind. I was holding on to so many things that were hurting me yet still trying to get them to work for me. If I had to give myself a name, I would have introduced myself as 'Broken'.

I was confused about my identity. I tried to medicate the pain with the fact that I was still able to hear the call from God. I wanted to throw myself into the work of the ministry rather than throwing myself at the feet of the Master who could fix this broken vessel. I thought that re-committing myself to church service and embarking on this new journey of "ministry" would fix the mess of a life I was living. I embodied pain, insecurity, inadequacy, hurt, disappointment and rejection...

I was sick. I knew that "they" knew that and that was my label. Sick, broken, busted, and disgusted.

A lot more transpired but we will leave that for another time. I just wanted to share some of the major events that took place in my developmental years. As an adult, I can now stand and say that it was good for me to be afflicted and that I'm glad for it all. My story is still one that is painted with many ups and downs, highs and lows, but I thank God for the journey.

I would compare my story to the woman with the issue of blood. You may think that's extreme but let me explain. There is a quote that I read that stated: "Until you heal the wounds of your past, you are going to bleed." That is exactly what the 20- to- 22-year-old Sarah was doing.... bleeding. I had open wounds in which blood oozed out and stained everyone and everything around me. There are three accounts of this woman's story in the Bible: in Matthew 9:20-22; Mark 5:25-34; and Luke 8:43-48, which I like best:

"And there was a woman who had a discharge of blood for twelve years, and though she had spent all her living on physicians, she could not be healed by anyone. She came up behind him and touched the fringe of his garment, and immediately her discharge of blood ceased. And Jesus said, "Who was it that touched me?" When all denied it, Peter said, "Master, the crowds surround you and are pressing in on you!" But Jesus said, "Someone touched me, for I perceive that power has gone out from me." And when the woman saw that she was not hidden, she came trembling, and falling down before him declared in the presence of all the people why she had touched him, and how she had been immediately healed. And he said to her, "Daughter, your faith has made you well; go in peace."

Three things stick out to me from her story: 1) She was cured after many attempts; 2) She was cured immediately; and 3) She was commended for her faith.

This story is known among Christians and non-Christians. Her story, her name, her reputation, and her struggle precede her. She, much like myself in the past, probably never had to introduce herself to anyone. I'm sure people did it for her, omitting or skipping over the part where she met Jesus and was sent on her way. I'm sure if this woman walked among us today people would talk more about her issue than her healing and deliverance. I spent a lot of my time "bleeding out", searching for healing from "the church" and instead finding ridicule and rejection. I questioned God about if the cycle would ever end. I had little to no strength to continue. I wanted to disappear. I was tired of being looked down upon, pushed aside and counted out.

But one day I heard news that the Messiah, the master of my messy situation, was walking by and I decided that I was tired of being tired. I reached out by faith and touched Him. I made a connection with Him, not church, not religion, not a shout, not another cover-up, but Him. Since then, my life has not been the same. The cycle dried up immediately and in exchange I received His virtue, power, strength and healing.

What can we learn from this woman with the issue of blood? She was so focused on her freedom that she did whatever it took to receive it. She decided that enough was enough and that she wanted peace. She overcame her fear of public or religious opinion. She didn't care about what people thought because they couldn't help her. She literally hit the floor by faith and reached out for her peace and received it on the day she met the Master. She assumed a certain posture before the Lord that would allow Him to do the work He needed to do.

When you feel like you have exhausted all options, that tight place will force what's on the inside of you to come out! Prayer and my faith are what kept me through the healing process. I wasn't always full of faith. The earlier parts of my Christian walk I was full of fluff! I had the word in me and had praying people around me but I didn't become filled until God changed my identity. In that season of complete brokenness, I took some time to really reach out and touch God. I sat with Him, leaned on Him, pressed into His presence, and depended on Him for life. I am so glad that today I stand a free woman, full of purpose, love, hope, strength and courage. When you actually meet Christ, everything about you changes, including the way you walk, talk, speak, and love.

Sister, my encouragement to you is that you choose not to suffer in silence. Choose not to succumb to your struggle and find the courage (even if you are in public ministry and you are going through) to step out or even step down for a season and seek God. Find Him on your knees. Surrender your life completely to your Savior. Take time to pray without pretension and without feeling that you have to perform before a God that already knows you intimately. The Potter wants to put you back together again. You are not so broken that you are beyond repair. Submit yourself to Jehovah Rapha, draw nigh to him, take the necessary steps on your journey, and prepare your heart to meet the Master.

Sarah Anderson is a community youth leader who serves under the covering of Pastor Richard & Lady Paula Brown at Kingsway Community Life Centre, Toronto, Canada. She is studying at Tyndale University and is pursuing a bachelor's degree in Human Services. She is passionately and fully committed to serving youth and women everywhere, taking the gospel message with her, and teaching practically about the love and transforming power of Jesus Christ.

WHAT I KNOW NOW!
BY SHINNINE NEWMAN

God's grace and mercy is the only reason why I am still here today. Sometimes I wonder where I would be if God had not delivered me from the foolishness of my younger years. I sit back and think about my life, about where I have been, and where I want to be. I know that I want to be able to use my experiences to help younger girls reach their full potential in God, and I know that I still have things that I need to work on. But I believe that as long as I continue to push, I will be able to reach my potential so God can really use me.

    I grew up in church but I was not always the innocent church girl that everyone expected me to be. Many of my experiences in life began when I started middle school. I was a small, very shy, skinny, non-athletic, and not very outgoing girl. I was bullied a lot, and later decided to bully others, which I now realize was not the way to solve my problems. I was very confused at that point in my life. I was confused with my sexuality, confused about my identity, and confused about who my real friends were. I was the kind of girl that would just fit in wherever I felt comfortable, and most of the times the places that I felt comfortable were not the places that I should've been. I wanted to be with a certain crowd because they acted a certain way and did things that I wanted to be a part of. I know now that just because you want to be in a certain position or in a certain group, doesn't mean that's where you should be.

As I got older, I made friends and I guess you can say they were the wrong kind of friends who exposed me to a lifestyle that wasn't Christian-friendly. They introduced me to different types of music, boys, and clothes. I found that the music and the clothes weren't major issues for me, but getting close to boys distracted me from my purpose. I wasn't the girl who went around doing things with a bunch of guys I didn't know, but I would make friends with them, try to get them to like me, and tell them things that they wanted to hear. I would talk to these boys, flirt with them, and tell them I would do things just because I wanted to fit in. Even though I would lead them on, I wouldn't actually do anything because I knew it was wrong and a small part of me still wanted to please God and my parents.

On March 20th 2006, the Saturday night of our Youth Conference, I finally decided to give my life to God through baptism. I felt like God knew it was time and the only thing stopping me was my shyness. It was almost a setup, where I was at the altar and just couldn't go back to my seat. I felt like if I turned around and went back to sit down I would be failing myself and disappointing God. I knew in my mind that I wanted to go to heaven to meet him, plus all of my friends were baptized and I wanted to be able to minister on the choir. So I decided to go for it. I really had nothing to lose. The only thing that was trying to hinder me was my shyness, but I didn't want that to be the reason I turned down the perfect opportunity my turnaround? So I did it. I was only 12 years old but it was a great feeling to finally have done it. I truly felt different, I felt like a weight was lifted. Yes! Now I don't have to feel bad when pastor tells the unsaved to go to the altar.

Not long after that I was in my seat one Saturday night at another Youth Conference that the Lord decided to fill me with the Holy Ghost. It happened quickly. I was glad it had finally happened.

Although I was finally filled and now singing on the youth choir, I still knew that I had to live a life according to God. I knew this meant that I had to let go of some of the clothes I wore and the music I listened to. It was rough, but I did it at least in front of church. I was holy, saved and sanctified only at church. Giving up certain music that I listened to wasn't that hard. Since I was on the choir I found pleasure in listening to gospel or Christian music because it was similar to what I listened to before. However, I was still a part of the wrong crowd at school, and being a Christian, and a born again Christian at that, it was a lot easier for people to judge me. I still wanted to be around boys and do what I had been doing. I still wanted to talk the same talk and walk the same walk as everyone else in school. I hung out with people that still influenced me in the wrong way. Every time I would say something or do something, I would get: "but aren't you a Christian?" or "I thought you were saved?" It upset me because I didn't think going to church would prevent me from doing what everyone else did. I was bored being a Christian; it felt like it limited me from having fun and being a teenager.

Starting high school was the roughest part of my walk with God. I got caught up in all the hype of everything that was around me and began to lose myself. This was the point in my life where I believe God brought me through things that I could surely learn from. I was Christian at church but not anywhere else. I acted like a Christian and people knew I was a Christian, but my actions were not weighed with good intentions.

I knew I was a child of God and I knew right from wrong, but I just didn't care about anything or anyone. I was very confused. I was caught up in pleasing my parents with my marks and playing the role in church but didn't really think about what God required of me. The confusion made me rebel against my parents and against certain Christian values. I was hanging around the wrong crowd, thinking thoughts that I should not have been thinking, or trying to gain appreciation and/or acceptance from the wrong people, including some who also considered themselves Christians.

I am grateful that I eventually had the strength to walk away when I felt like my soul and my Christianity was in danger. Although it took the worst-case scenario for me to leave these ungodly relationships, God truly extended his grace towards me, and helped me to fight for my life.

I thought learning how to walk away from non-Christians would be my last test. However, I got into a relationship with someone that I thought was the answer to a prayer. A boyfriend was the last thing that I should've been praying for but I did. Unlike the other relationships, I hoped this one would be meaningful since I prayed for it. I should've just realized there was an emptiness in me that needed to be filled.

I tried to hold on to a relationship that I knew in my heart wasn't going to last or prosper. That emptiness in me just wanted to be filled and I guess you can say I got desperate. So many things tried to break me from this person but I thought that it was the enemy messing with my heart. Now that I am older, I realize that God was trying to get my attention to let me know that He was the only one who could fill my emptiness.

Once that relationship ended, I was emotionally spent. Other relationships with so-called friends ended at the same time. My heart was broken and the void in me grew. All I could do was cry myself to sleep or eat. Nothing could cheer me up. At school, I just by myself sat at a table like a loner. I didn't have interest in anything, and felt like my life was meaningless. I always had something or someone with me to occupy me or distract me. I was really alone, I felt dependent, and I had low self-esteem. At this point, I didn't think I was good enough to do anything. I wasn't very talkative or outgoing. I was so broken but didn't even realize how bad it was.

I became depressed through the remainder of my first year of university. I realized I needed help. I eventually made two amazing friends who tried everything they could to lift my spirits and help me overcome the heartache so I could move on. I had to look into my heart and get to the root of the issue.

My relationship with God wasn't strong enough to help me get better and stay better. I had people who told me to pray about my situation, and I did. However, I prayed the way people told me to pray, and fasted the way people told me to fast. My relationship with God was not personal. I realize now that I went to people for help instead of going straight to the Creator.

After a while, I decided to work out my walk with God and fix my relationship with Him on my own. I looked up different woman in the Bible and learned from them. I thought this would help me grow spiritually, to pray more and to fast more, and it did. I learned how to pray when I'm down but also when I'm happy. I learned how to trust and depend on God.

During this time, I was distracted, and I fell, but I was able to know when and how to get out of the situation and to get back in line.

Through this time in my life, things came to drag me away from where I needed to be in God. Sometimes it was just frustration, fear, lack of faith, or that empty feeling. I learned how to guard my heart and control my emotions. God is constantly revealing things to me whether it be through school, work, YouTube, or people He sends in my life. There is something out there that God wants me to do and I need to be ready to do that, and I've learned that the only way I'll truly be ready is if I guard my heart.

Despite the rollercoasters of life over the years, I've been truly blessed. God has countered the negative with positive times to guard my heart and my mind. He has allowed me to meet new people and make new friends who really want to see me grow. They rejoice with me in my good times and lift me up in my bad times. I've truly grown as a Christian and as a woman of God. It is only by His grace that I am able to share my story.

Shinnine Newman is a student at the University of Toronto. Her dream is to be a successful broadcast journalist. She sings on two choirs at her church and occasionally on the praise and worship team. On her YouTube channel, she addresses women lifestyle issues. She plans to continue to please God and be a mentor for young girls.

PURE GOLD
BY RUTH NAOMI MITCHELL

In today's society, choosing to live as a Godly woman is not the biggest hit in the popularity market, especially as a young woman. The world defines what a woman should be, what she should look like, and how she should live. A true Godly woman is often tossed aside, labeled, rejected, and even judged because she doesn't fit that definition. Nowhere in society is a pedestal set for a "Jesus follower and believer" so separating oneself from the world comes with many fights and territories. Every day is a constant battle, battling with self, battling the righteous way of living life, and battling society's perception of you. I am thankful to be able to share some of my life experiences as a woman that has been saved by grace.

Saved All Your Life

Have you been saved all your life? No one has been saved all their life. For the word of God declares in Psalm 51:5: *"For I was born a sinner--yes, from the moment my mother conceived me."* Many women struggle with a defective feeling of being saved all their lives. I was raised apostolic, which meant my life schedule was very predictable and looked like the following: Sunday - church; Wednesday - Bible study or youth service; and Thursday and Friday - maybe choir practice.

How many of you can agree with me that people have placed you in a predictable box because they know that you have been a church girl all your life? They assume you've been saved all of your life and you're expected to never make mistakes. I declare that today is your day of being delivered from the "Saved All Your Life Defect". Yes, you were born into your faith. Yes, you speak in tongues and are baptized in Jesus' name. Yes, you sing on the choir. Yes, you are an active member and partaker in the ministry of God. Yes, you are a Godly woman. Yes, you will make mistakes.

The Bible says: *"For all have sinned, and come short of the glory of God."* (Rom. 3:23) Living in this society as a Godly woman doesn't exempt you from coming short of God's glory. This first step to living as a Godly woman is simply to acknowledge that you will make mistakes. We will be women of standard, women who follow after God's heart, and be virtuous as we pursue God. But we will also make mistakes.

What do you do after you've made a mistake? Many of us beat ourselves up because of our mistakes. The funny thing is some of these mistakes are far in our past. Many of us can't forgive ourselves for things that we have done as teenagers and it prevents us from operating effectively as Godly women. Today, I declare healing over your past mistakes and we will no longer allow people to categorize us by our mistakes. Many times, I've had to walk out of the category in which others placed me. If you listen to today's society, you find yourself pleasing them rather than pleasing God.

Women of God, walk out of the in which category in which others have placed you and turn your mistakes into testimonies. The reason why I am the woman that I am today is because of my mistakes and learning to turn them into my testimonies. I truly believe that when I chose to live for God, I automatically signed up for a battle. I have failed many battles... the battle with fornication, the battle with lust, the battle with needing a man to be in my life, and the battle of fear. I can stand today and declare that I have overcome all these battles, many of which tormented me for years. I have gone to the altar countless times and walked away thinking I was delivered, and the next day I was doing the same things I declared to God that I would never do again. Do not allow your mistakes to dictate to you. I never forgot who God created me to be. I never forgot my purpose and the ministry God gave me.

Oftentimes, our mistakes cloud our thoughts, our minds, and our perception of how we view ourselves. I declare to you that mistakes will not cloud your perceptions because you are who God says you are. Your mistakes are in the past and they shall remain in your past and they will not hold on to your future. Change these mistakes into your testimonies and be free, in Jesus name. See your mistakes as an opportunity to do something for God. I have learned to use all of my shortcomings as tools, sources, and opportunities to minister to women across the world, some of whom I mentor. God has given me many platforms to host women's seminars and He has graciously appointed me as the First Lady of a dynamic ministry. I say all this to say, living as a Godly woman in this society isn't easy. The pressure of living in this world is intense, but as long as you accept that mistakes are normal and turn those experiences into testimonies for God to receive the Glory, you will never regret the process. I often ask myself, "How could I have counselled this person if I didn't gain that exact experience?" I am a believer that the Holy Ghost teaches us all things, but I must say through my experiences and the guidance of God I have been able to walk effectively in my ministry as a Godly woman.

My Second Chance

God gave me a second chance to overcome my fears. He gave me a second chance to live for Him as a Godly woman. He gave me a second chance to restore my ministry. He definitely gave me a second chance when I became Mrs. Mitchell. I use the figurative term "second chance" when describing God's grace towards me but our God is truly a God of many chances. No matter what we have done in this walk as women who desire to live for Him, He is always there to forgive us. God always finds a route to channel us right back to His purpose once we are willing to be led by Him. Every Godly woman should desire to give their life totally to God so that He will lead you according to His purpose. I strongly believe this is the reason why I am who I am in Him. No matter how many times I turned left on God, I was always willing to have Him control and lead me at the end of the day. I was able to be restored by Him. In 2 Cor. 12:9, it states: *"But he said to me, "My grace is sufficient for you, for my power is made perfect in weakness. Therefore, I will boast all the more gladly about my weaknesses, so that Christ's power may rest on me."*

My most powerful combats were when I was deep in my weakness. I remember one day, upon the preparation of a very important event in my life, one of the leaders sensed that I had the spirit of fear. Once she realized fear had taken over my mind, she immediately confronted my fears and took authority as a woman of God and commanded fear to leave me. She spoke to me and declared my purpose in my life. It was in my weakness of this experience that I found strength. I found the strength to conquer fear and I received the power of God that continues to rest upon me. I believe my spiritual gifts were amplified through this experience. Ladies, know that God's grace is sufficient for you. In times of weakness, He shall be your strength. Always allow God to steer your life because His power is made perfect in your weakness.

I am very thankful to God for giving me a second chance to live for Him as a Godly woman. Many of us do not understand the seriousness of living as a Godly woman. Many of us were brought up in church all our lives or for those who got saved later in life, we all assume that we are Godly now and that's it. I must say that having our first experience of receiving the gift of the Holy Ghost and being baptized in Jesus' name is just the beginning of being a Godly woman. It is up to us to live the life of a Godly woman. Having one foot in the church and the other foot in the world is not being a Godly woman. It is important that our lives reflect holiness, godliness, righteousness, and that we live in modesty. When we walk in this life, it is crucial that we represent the King that we are living for.

My challenges as a teen caused me to waver in my Godly living. I struggled to be separated from this world. The peer pressure in high school had me confused. While in high school I would succumb to peer pressure with how I dressed and even with how I behaved towards my parents. After high school, I struggled to build my own identity in university. When I say God gave me a second chance to live for Him as a woman, He sure did. I was never the type to hit the clubs but I was becoming desensitized to the Godly principles that I was taught at an early age. Everything about me was slowly slipping: the music I played was so wrapped up in love. Every love song I could find to play, I played. The radio stations I listened to were my back up source for when I was tired of my CD selections. I was wrapped up with lust through the songs I listened to in my car. These songs not only impacted how I dressed but affected how I acted as a woman. If this is who you are, I am here to tell you that you can still be delivered. The process of overcoming this wasn't easy and it took discipline. I love to dance, and music gives me a creative vision. As a Godly woman, you have to remind yourself that you are God's property so I had to remind myself that I am not my own. The word of God declares in 1 Cor. 6:19-20: *"What? Know ye not that your body is the temple of the Holy Ghost which is in you, which ye have of God, and ye are not your own? For ye are bought with a price: therefore glorify God in your body, and in your spirit, which are God's."* Ladies, protect your body and your spirit. Be very careful of what you allow in. Since God gave me a second chance to live for Him, I was able to give up the desires of my flesh and trade it in for the desires of wanting a relationship with God by being a true woman of God.

I am very thankful that God always saw the best in me, even when I was at my worst. Many times I couldn't comprehend how I got to the place in life where I couldn't function in my calling. Without elaborating in great detail, I feel the need to caution any woman that needs to hear this. When God says to move, move without hesitation. When God says get up and move forward so that I can provide increase, do just that without questioning Him. I declare that everyone woman that is reading this will have the spirit of boldness. Women, learn to be bold for God. Many of us have been given gifts but because we refuse to be bold, they can't manifest. I sat at a place in my life for years being trapped, not being able to pursue what I had been called to do for God. I was mostly afraid of what people would think of me if I did something out of the ordinary. But can I tell you pleasing people can trap you. You can be so busy pleasing people until you find yourself being trapped by what others think of you. I was trapped for years, until God gave me a second chance to restore my ministry, to restore who I was called to be in Him. The very moment I decided to move forward in life, and in ministry, God began to open doors for me. The restoration process did not happen overnight but I knew that God hadn't forgotten me. I sat for almost a year during my transition and restoration not being as active in church. While God gave me rest, He was restoring me for greater.

The word of God declares in Prov. 18:16: *"A man's gift maketh room for him, and bringeth him before great men."* One day, one of my dear friends extended an invitation to go to Guyana on a missions trip. Without hesitation, I told her that I would be delighted to join the team from Florida. Ladies, God words are true. Your gifts will make room for you, and bring you before great men. Before I left for Guyana in late April 2013, I made up in my mind that I would accept what God had called me to do in His Kingdom. I watched God restore my ministry even before I could see the manifestations of it in the natural. While I was in Guyana, I remember saying to myself that this is what I want to do for God; I want to travel on missions trips, I want to be a minister, and a carrier of His glory. It was right there and then, I made up in my mind that the path that I was taking in life spiritually and physically was not the plans that God had for me.

Amazingly, I met the man of my dreams in Guyana. He was also a part of the team who was sent to there to serve. The very moment I surrendered my life completely to God, and accepted my calling in Him, He blessed me with my husband. I never went to Guyana with the intentions of finding a husband, but God never hesitated to grant me the desires of my heart. I wish to tell my complete story on how I met my husband, and the experiences that we had before we became one. God, I thank you for giving me a chance to be with a true man of God, the one you allowed me to call husband. I met "the one" in July 2007 at a church camp in Florida, and never would have thought that he would be "the one" and he felt the same way. Seven years later, on April 30th 2013, I met "the one" on that missions trip. On April 12th 2014, he finally became the one forever. Only God could have blessed me in the way He did, when He did it.

I have gone through hurts, pains, aches, hardship, and have suffered many broken hearts, but God kept me. My God kept me because I was always persistent. Even though I failed Him countless times, I never gave up. I always knew that I was a woman of purpose, called to a higher calling. I am standing right now as a testimony that God can take filth and turn it into pure gold. Sometimes, I reflect and I still can't believe how good God has been to me. God told me at a tender age that I am called to lead His people, and He said to me that I was different. Although I have fallen many times, I never doubted my calling. I have always stood up after a fall. Today, I am now a proud pastor's wife and I enjoy standing behind the man of God. I do believe that greater is coming. Ladies, don't give up on God. The journey will be worth it.

Ruth Naomi Mitchell is the daughter of Donald and Orinthia James. She serves as youth pastor and first lady, alongside her husband Pastor Damien Mitchell at Overcomers Tabernacle of the New Life Community Church Internal (N.L.C.C.I) in Edmonton, under the ministry of our overseer of all the New Lifes Pastor Andrew Steele. Ruth was born and raised in Kingston, Jamaica, moved to the United States and currently resides in Edmonton, Canada. I am simply a believer and a follower of the Lord Jesus Christ who is simply saved by Grace.

THE JOURNEY
BY KETURAH MORRIS

When I was a little girl, I struggled with extreme low self-esteem. It was an incessant feeling that constantly threatened to rear its ugly head whenever it suited and by any means necessary. It came to the surface during times of despair, times of questionability, times of loneliness and times of invisibility. There was a constant war with this prevailing feeling of depression and my weak attempt to reaffirm my own self-worth. I was not strong enough to determine whether or not I was good enough or if I was just a stand-in for another worthy candidate. I had not come to the full acknowledgement of the immense importance and value of who I was without any added extra 'stuff' in between. I had not met the true essence of myself that was to be wrapped up in this perfect Creator that I had been brought up to know.

Let me break it down…

I grew up in a family that was in the 'limelight' by way of the ministry. My father's father was a bishop, my mother's father was a bishop, and my own father is a bishop. My family has been called to pastoral ministry before my own conception. Unbeknownst to me, ministry was also the road I too was meant to travel.

Having been reared in the church spotlight, my life was under constant scrutiny. The way I dressed, spoke, and lived, were being watched and ultimately judged. It became too much for me to handle. I thought to myself, "I am a good kid!" To be frank, I was not the girl that went to parties, had boyfriends, drank or experimented with drugs. I held my life together, or so I thought. There was a deep need inside of me to be seen for who I really was, not to be judged, not to be under constant watch, but to be accepted for what was inside of me.

In every woman, there is a deep-seated need to be seen. Every woman wants recognition for just being her. Mothers want to be thanked for cooking dinner for her family. Little girls want to be told that they are beautiful as they dress themselves in mommy's clothes and makeup. From the moment a young girl is born, she is dressed in pretty pink, frilly, sparkly clothing. She is put on display for all to love and shower her with affection. Family members will come from far to look at the beautiful baby, with her soft curls, her precious smile and pretty little dresses. We produce a system of 'oohing' and 'aahing' so that we can gaze at this wondrous creation made by God.

Once the little baby gets older, she prances around the house, strutting herself for all to see, and with every swish of her little skirt, she begs all: "Look at me. Am I not pretty?" She wants to be admired for her beauty. She wants all to be aware of her presence. It is this same deep sentiment that I too clamored for. I wanted all to be aware of my presence. In my heart, I was screaming out to the world: "Do you think I'm beautiful? Can you see me? Am I enough?"

Recognition and love, I felt, had evaded me. I knew my family loved me, like really loved me, but my heart was yearning for something beyond that. I couldn't put a name to it or formulate its importance to me, but I needed it. I had to be loved because what else is stronger than love? You know that deep kind of love that does not need to be questioned or proven? The kind of love that is self-sacrificing, unconditional, and relentless? I felt like I hadn't yet experienced so deep a love and I was unwilling to live without it.

Upon recognition of what I was really missing, I searched and begged for it, hoping it would come and whisk me away, and help smother the constant depression and self-deprecatory way of thinking that was beginning to take over my mind. After some time, I felt no change. There was no immediate eradication of the pain that had surrounded my heart. Things were slowly getting worse. I began hiding from the world. I sheltered myself from everything around me. I comforted my pain with my pain. I made no attempt to come out of my cave of seclusion. It was me against the world. I had no time for my family and ultimately no time for God. Because I grew up in church, I knew about God, and I even thought I had a real relationship with Him. I attended service like I was supposed to. I did everything by the book just to evade any stares and incessant lectures of concern. I avoided people at any cost. I was mad at the world and I wanted no part in it. That's when things took a turn for the worst.

I remember it like it was yesterday. This day was no different than any other. I had barricaded myself in my room, subjected to my own self-loathing ideas and prevailing depressive actions. Thought after thought ravished my mind, day after day until that moment they had taken control of me. I found myself on my bedroom floor, sobbing until I heard one thought that dominated the others: "No one cares about you. Take your life. No one will miss you."

Through the tears and loud gasps for air, I suddenly stopped and sat there, reveling in this fraudulent lie that I was an outcast, forsaken by all around me and unloved by the 'man upstairs'. It was time to end the pain. Time to deafen the thoughts that sought refuge in my mind and find peace. I had come to grips that taking my life was indeed necessary. I lifted myself off of the ground and took one last look at my room, the place that had been my sanctuary for so long. I opened my bedroom window, took the screen off of its hinges, and stepped out onto the roof to take my own life. Once on the roof, I followed the voice further onto the edge. I had made up my mind to take the leap to my death and end it all. But before I could, I had to make sure that there were no onlookers around that would try to halt my quest for freedom. As I looked around to the left and right, I didn't see anybody. There were no school children playing outside, no pedestrians, not a soul. I was free and clear to take my final leap. My feet moved forward, slowly inching closer and closer to the edge. One more step and I would be at peace. One more step and all my troubles would be over. I would not be seen or even heard. I would be gone – free.

As I lifted my foot off the ground for the last step, I heard a strong voice yell, "Katie!" I shook with fear because I checked to make sure no one was around. And there still wasn't. The voice rang clear once more, "Katie!" It was as if I was being summoned from far away. I hesitantly replied, "Yes?" The voice responded back just as clear as before, "What are you doing? Don't you know that I love you? Don't you know that you are my daughter? I have plans for you. Come back inside."

In that moment, more than any moment I have ever experienced, the tears flowed down my face ever so freely. Finally the tears that came down my face were not tears of pain and deep seated hurt but of this newfound peace, which was persistent in invading my heart and was able to overcome the negative inner thoughts that brought me to the roof in the first place. The peace came because the King of Kings, the very Creator of the world, the mender of broken hearts and the designer of all things beautiful – which included me. He stooped down from his majestic home in Heaven and took time out to save little ole me, the same person who forsook His teachings and ignored his word to suit my own purposes and to prolong my own pain. Why would He choose to come down and prevent me from taking my own life? Why would He choose to save the life of someone who was invisible to the world and mattered very little? He chose to save me the first time by sending his only son to Calvary and dying on an old cross to take on my sins, the very sins that needed to be covered with grace before I had even committed them. He already decided to save me by giving me an opportunity to accept him as my personal savior and take on His name as His daughter.

I am reminded of the scripture John 3:16-17 that says: *"For God so loved the world that he gave his only begotten Son, that whosoever believeth in him should not perish, but have everlasting life. For God sent not his Son into the world to condemn the world; but that the world through him might be saved."* He not only loved me but wanted to save me by that same love and not condemn me! Wow, what a powerful message that was hidden in the word that as a little girl finally hit home and gravitated to my soul.

I finally understood that the feelings of emptiness and invisibility was because I felt unseen by the world and my loved ones, but it was from my Jesus. I desperately needed Him to see me. I needed to know that if I asked Him with my twirling skirt and pretty sparkly slippers, "Daddy, do you think I am pretty?" he would respond with a resounding applause and say, "Yes! Of course my daughter, you are beautiful. You are enough. I see you!"

And when He pushed me from the edge of the roof, He did just that. He reminded me that He did not just see me in that moment but He had seen me all my life. From the moment I was conceived in my mother's womb, He had seen me.

This time in my life has been essential. It has catapulted me on a journey that has forever changed the course of my life. It was needful for me to get so low that only the Savior would be able to catch me and lift me back up. This journey has had some major bumps in the road that has sometimes challenged my faith, but it has never brought me so low again past the point of no return, and for that I am grateful.

Sometimes in our lives, we need to be reminded of God's love for us. Unfortunately, some of us have to hit rock bottom before completely coming to the full knowledge of who God is and how much we need Him. In those 'near edge' moments when we're close to taking that last step, God calls us by name. Sadly, some don't hear him, and it is too late. I wanted to open this part of my life to the rest of the world because I believe that through this God is using me to be his voice before someone else takes that last step. He may not speak audibly like He did with me that day on my roof, but He speaks in many other ways. It is up to us to open not only our ears, but to open our hearts and minds and be ready to hear from Him. He loves us enough to take the time out to remind us that we are not alone on this journey. Like those footsteps in the sand, He is right there with us.

In the parable of the lost sheep, in which Jesus spoke to some tax collectors and sinners Luke 15:3-6, it says: *"Then Jesus told them this parable: "Suppose one of you has a hundred sheep and loses one of them. Doesn't he leave the ninety-nine in the open country and go after the lost sheep until he finds it? And when he finds it, he joyfully puts it on his shoulders and goes home. Then he calls his friends and neighbors together and says, 'Rejoice with me; I have found my lost sheep."*

We are the lost sheep and Jesus is the shepherd that leaves the others to come and find us. He is looking for you and calling out your name. Open your heart because He loves you. Remember, "You are beautiful. You are enough, and he sees you!"

Keturah Morris is the daughter of Bishop and First Lady Morris. She serves in ministry in different capacities. She is co-musical director, head choir mistress, and head praise leader. She also serves as the Singles Ministry and Big Sisters Ministry coordinator at her local church.

I WILL NEVER FORGET THE DAY I ALMOST LOST MY MIND
BY NASHARA PEART

It was a Wednesday night. I was standing in a rehearsal for my university's gospel choir, just about to lead the corporate devotion and prayer for the group. As choir members took a few minutes to greet one another and settle in, I stood alone, thinking about struggles I would have to return to once the reprieve of choir practice had come to an end. I thought about my seemingly never-ending pile of studying and assignments, and how I was at the point of not caring whether or not I ever completed them. I reflected upon the campus ministry that I was leading, largely on my own, because of miscommunication and differences in priorities between myself and the other group leaders. I thought about the relationship I was considering even though I knew it would only be damaging to me in the end. I also worried about the nagging feeling I had been having lately, one that kept trying to convince me I was letting God down.

As the thoughts lingered in my mind, I began laughing, almost uncontrollably. A friend asked me if I was okay, but I did not have enough control over my body or my mind to express what I was feeling. In that moment, I thought my sanity was slipping away. It seemed like I was working so hard at everything that was going wrong, and giving up looked easy. I so desperately wanted to choose something easy.

I thank God almost every day that He did not let me choose what I thought was the easy way. Just before I completely gave into my feelings, God reminded me that nothing could separate me from His love. In the space of a few seconds, I went from tired, weak and vulnerable, to immensely grateful that I had the Lord on my side to snatch my mind back from the demon that was assigned to take it from me. I learned one of my most valuable lessons in that moment: God is faithful. He has never doubted my ability to overcome because He built me with the DNA of a conqueror.

I did not always have the connection with God that saved me that day. Having grown up in church, I knew the expectations of a Christian, but I did not always make the effort to have a personal relationship with God. I remember a time when I was standing at the altar following a preacher's message. As I looked around at those seeking the Holy Spirit or reaching out in prayer, I thought to myself that it all seemed foolish. I did not want to be at the altar and I did not want to be encouraged to pray. At the time it seemed to me like I was wasting my time, and so was everyone else. To say the least, I spent the majority of my adolescence in an indifferent state. I thank God I was sober enough at various points to make the decision to get baptized, and then to seek the Holy Spirit, but outside of those pockets of time in my youth, God was not my focus.

It was not until I was confronted with the reality of moving away from home to begin university that I really began to take Christ seriously. As I look back on it now, I am so glad the Lord shook me awake when He did. A university campus is not an easy place to navigate without the direction of Christ. Had I remained in my indifferent state, I cannot even imagine what might have befallen me. As I learned to steer my way in a new city, a new school, and a new home on my own, my dependence on God to be my strength and encouragement grew immensely. During this time, God demonstrated His faithfulness, standing with me in a time when loneliness was a real threat. Surrounded by thousands of new students and even on-campus roommates, I struggled to find a place where I fit in. God had it that the only place I felt comfortable for the first few weeks in my new city was in church. The saints welcomed me with so much warmth and love that I began to regard my new church family as a safety net in a time when I felt I was struggling to keep my head above water. I don't even think the saints knew it, but they loved me back to a place where I felt okay to explore my new school, speak up boldly in my classes, and make connections with people that I knew the Lord placed in my life for special reasons.

The rest of my time in university flew by. My on-campus experiences had their part in my transformation to living the life of a Godly woman, but it was my newfound devotion to ministry and seeking out the will of God for my life that changed me in the deepest parts of my soul. There is a part in all of us that wants God, and during my four years of undergraduate studies, that part of me awoke and craved food and nourishment more than it ever had in my life. I realized during that time that I needed God to survive. As I led the campus ministry group and interacted with students from diverse backgrounds, I began to appreciate more and more just how blessed I was to have a relationship with God as I navigated the trials of being a student.

It was not until the conclusion of my undergraduate studies that I stumbled into another of the most challenging periods of my life. After finishing school in April 2013, I was without a job. I had rent and bills that needed to be taken care of, and no matter how hard I tried I was unable to find work. My parents were also supporting my brother and sister, each of whom was also out of the house in university, so I felt extra pressure to find work so I could alleviate some of the new demand I had placed on them. I handed out about one hundred resumes, and with each one, I felt more and more defeated. My roommates were working and in summer school at the time so I spent most of the day alone in our apartment. There were several days I never left my room. I did not want to get up to face the day when I did not feel it would yield any fruit. I began to shut down. I was not communicating well with the people I lived with because I did not want to talk about how I felt: that somehow I was failing at trusting God to help me. I watched most of the beautiful summer days through the window, too cast down in my spirit to even venture outdoors.

It took me many months until I was finally able to hear the message God wanted me to understand; He wanted to spend this alone time with me. He had detached me from work and school because He wanted all of my time. When I finally tuned into His voice and began spending time with Him, things quickly began to improve. I was able to realize how deep I had fallen into a depressed state, how I had alienated myself from my friends and family, and how much beauty I let slip past me as I spent my days hidden away inside. In total, I spent eight months out of the year with no job. It was not until the month of December during my daily devotion that I told God I really did not want the year to end without having a job. Shortly thereafter, I received a call for an interview. On December 31, I got the call to say I had been selected for the position. The year did not end before the Lord fulfilled my specific request. Although I had experienced His faithfulness so many times before, this time really broke me. He was faithful when I was not. He was constant while I was wavering. He was patient while I thought I was falling apart, waiting for me to believe He would never allow that to happen.

About a month into the new job, as I was thinking about the events of the previous year, I was inspired to write a poem. The words flowed easily as I expressed what my spirt had learned about God. I grew to love Him so much more in that time, and as I've continued to draw closer to Him, I constantly feel my heart swell with each new revelation of his mercy, and of the unmerited favour. I know the only way I can survive as a Godly woman in this world is because of the fact that God is literally holding my life together. I have been tested since, but my heart is resolved to trust God in every situation and believe that He will never let me down.

My Lesson

God is faithful.

There is an awe-inspiring, life-changing, mind-altering, seemingly complicated

simplicity

hidden in the fact that

God is faithful.

He never forsakes us, never stops loving us, never leaves the righteous begging bread

even though we deserve death.

He understands every single tear we've ever cried, and every moan we've ever uttered

even though we don't take enough time to stop and listen to Him.

God's patience is perfect.

His meek heart towards us is entirely unmerited.

His provision is profoundly underserved

although desperately required.

His grace is far more than sufficient.

His love is complete.

There is an awe-inspiring, life-changing, mind-altering, seemingly complicated

simplicity

hidden in the fact that

God is faithful.

Nashara Peart was born and raised in Ontario, Canada, and is the second of three children. Her home church assembly is Triumphant Church of Jesus Christ (Apostolic), under the leadership of Bishop Evon Nunes. Since moving away to begin her university career, she has attended Apostolic Ark Ministries under the direction of Bishop Kenroy Morris. Nashara is a part of several ministries including the choir and praise teams, drama ministry, and being a mentor to young girls. Nashara is also the co-founder of the Sisters in Praise ministry. Nashara completed an Honours Bachelor of Arts in Sociology at McMaster University before pursuing a diploma in Public Relations. Her future goals include being a criminal lawyer with a focus on juvenile justice. In her spare time, Nashara enjoys reading, travelling, and spending time with her loved ones.

THE STORY BEHIND MY PRAISE
BY SHARON EDMUND-BROWN

My life has been quite the journey filled with many hurdles, obstacles, hills to climb, and valleys to cross, but by the grace of God, I have made it and will continue to make it on this journey. I pray that my story will help you to find your hope, strength, and peace in God.

As I reflect on my life today, I have proven that Jesus is a deliverer from sin, a burden bearer when the burdens get too heavy, a healer when you have been broken into pieces, a forgiver of sin, and a provider. I have also proven that it doesn't not matter how messed up your past has been, God can and will make something beautiful out of your life. For someone like myself, I came to Jesus as I was, weary, worn, lost, sad, battered, tormented and confused, but Jesus looked beyond all of that and cleaned me up. Who knew that I would become a Godly woman? I had no idea that this was my future. I had no idea that God would turn my life around the way He did because the path I took to get there is a path that could have and should have led to death. Instead, I received life and that more abundantly.

It started in the early 1980s when I left Jamaica as a teenager, and went to Canada with high hopes of going to university and making something out of my life. I had dreams of becoming a lawyer. My parents spent a lot of money for me to attend prestigious schools in Jamaica so that I could receive the best education possible, and my hopes were to continue on this journey upon my arrival in Canada; but this was not my reality. Instead of pursing my educational goals, I began working in a factory in order to survive. I tried to never complain and make the best of the circumstances, and I was always a happy person who never allowed the hardships of life to get the best of me. I thought this was an amazing opportunity, and so I made the best of it. I fit in where I could as a new immigrant youth to Canada and I did what I needed to survive. I continued to work different jobs here and there, went to church with my family, and went to school at night because I still had hopes of becoming a lawyer. That was my dream. That is why I came to Canada. It was supposed to be my reality. Although the obstacles continued, I fought with a smile on face because deep down inside I knew it would get better… or would it?

My life transitioned a few years later when I met my first love, well at least I thought it was love. Because I came to Canada so young, I believed that there were a lot things I missed out on, love, that parental love that every child needs. As a result, I lacked guidance in what I should have been looking for in a partner and ended up in an abusive relationship which I did not leave because I thought he loved me. I thank God for the two precious gifts that relationship produced, my daughter, Jessica, and my son, Jahmar. But my life with this man was filled with physical and emotional abuse.

I remember it like it was yesterday. I was standing in the kitchen weighing in at about 110 pounds and pregnant with Jessica. I was a small little thing. He came in and asked me for some hot chocolate, and as I was in the process of making it, we exchanged some unkind words which resulted in me having two broken legs. Yes, he broke my legs with a crate of beer bottles, while I was pregnant with my daughter. I spent an entire day just sitting in the same spot crying because I could not move.

Unfortunately, that was not my only abusive relationship. In my next relationship, I almost lost my life. He held that gun to my head and kicked me in my stomach when I was pregnant with my last child, Jahron, who is a miracle. The enemy tried to cancel the births of all my children, but before God even formed them, they were covered and destined for greatness, and no devil in hell could stop that.

Ladies, when I look over the crazy path my life took, I realize the hand of God was with me through it all. I could have lost my baby and I could have lost my life, but His mercies kept me. Even though I was not saved and had no idea what my life would become, I am convinced that God's presence was with me. During that time in my life, my children and I spent a lot of time in shelters because of the domestic abuse. My children also grew up without their father in their lives, and being mother and father for them was not easy. That in itself was a journey. I was never taught motherhood or had an instruction manual on how to do this, but by the grace of God I made it through, and I tried my best to provide for my children.

In 1996, I ended up in a beautiful Island called Antigua. Many people have never heard about this place and neither did I, but I wanted a fresh start. I wanted to do it for my children and for myself. I wanted my children to have what I didn't have, a healthy home, an education, and the ability to be whatever they wanted to be. I had no idea what was going to happen when I went to Antigua but the Lord had great things in store. I always wondered how I ended up there. I know the steps of a good man are ordered by God. It was in Antigua that I got baptized in Jesus' name and received the Holy Ghost. That was the brand new start that God gave me and I am grateful. However, before I became a Christian, there were other struggles that I had to deal with such as my addiction to alcohol. It was so serious that I would drink myself to sleep, or blast music, drink my alcohol and dance the night away... by myself. I drank to numb the pain. I drank because I felt like I had no hope. I drank because it was relaxing and I knew that by morning it wear off and I'd be back on my hustle and ready to get my kids ready for school and whatever else the day would bring.

I should have died from serious liver disease because of my addiction, but God didn't allow me to die from the ungodly lifestyle that I lived. Another area of my life that controlled me was that I lived like a Rahab by night and lived like a working class woman in the day. In other words, I would do what I had to do so that my children and I had food, shelter and clothing. I didn't love these men and these men didn't love me, but once again my children had to eat and the bills had to be paid. I was never proud of this area of my life, but I will never be ashamed of my past. I am the woman who I am today because my past and I am able to encourage other women who have been through similar situations. Funny enough, I remember before I got saved a prominent minister told me that God did not have any use for me because of my past and because of where I was at that time. Can you imagine a 'man of God' speaking such things over your life? Of course, at the time I believed him, and really did not see God turning my life around the way He did. But I am so grateful that God is not like man. He looked beyond all of my faults, my lifestyle, my hurt, my pain and my brokenness and saw that I needed a Saviour. I believe that God will allow us to go through situations so that in the end He will get the glory. I look at David who was an adulterer, and yet a man after God's own heart; Rahab who was a prostitute and yet ended up in the lineage of Christ; and Noah who was an alcoholic yet he was obedient to the voice of God. At the end of the day, they were all used by God. Once again women of God, He can turn your darkness into day. All you have to do is trust Him.

I got saved in 1999 and oh what a change! I remember that day vividly. My children attended church with one of our neighbors so I figured I should see the place where they were and the bus driver, the late Minister Paterson, kept inviting me. I had no intentions of letting go my lifestyle, no intentions on being baptized, and certainly no intentions on being used by God. I mean, after all, God didn't have any use for me, right? Ironically, the message that day was, "God has use for you." The man of God looked me in the face, told me that I needed to be loosed and that God has use for me. Talk about God turning my situation around! As the preacher spoke, something got a hold of me and I was convicted to give my life to the Lord. Before I knew it, I filled with the Holy Ghost and singing on the choir!

One year later, I got married. God blessed me with an awesome man of God. I certainly did not expect this but I was grateful. My children needed a father and God sent them one. This man of God taught my children what it meant to have a Godly heritage, how to pray, how to read their Bibles, how to fear the Lord, and the importance of church and Sunday school. He was also an important father figure, especially in the life of my boys who needed a positive male influence in their lives. I salute this man of God who significantly contributed to the spiritual heritage of my children which is helping them today.

Our marriage lasted 12 years until everything suddenly fell apart, and then came a divorce. This was a very difficult time, both for me and for my children. At the time of the divorce, I was living in Florida then moved to another state, where I lost everything that I worked for and had to start over. I was tired of moving and tired of starting over. During this time, my two eldest children moved back to Canada in order to pursue their education and my youngest child was with me. I had no family, no job, and very little support. Things were falling apart. To make it worse, my youngest son started rebelling and it was difficult to handle on my own. Then I got very sick. During the sickness, I didn't think I was going to make it out alive, and I was tired of fighting. I could not believe that I was lying in a hospital bed, at the point of death, not able to help myself, my children were away, and it felt like hell was breaking lose in my life.

I asked God, "Why did you take me out of the world to allow me to go through all of this pain?" Ladies, I came to a point where I felt like giving up. I was tired of fighting. I had been fighting all of my life. However, through much prayer, fasting and the strong support that I received on this journey I have been able to overcome.

Going through a divorce is not easy and without a doubt the enemy knows how to remind you of your weaknesses. I started struggling with loneliness, fleshly desires, brokenness, and looking for love in the wrong places. I struggled to stay alive spiritually because of my troubled past, and I did things that were not aligned with the word of God. The whole time, I was looking for an easy way out and smooth sailing. I'm glad I never gave. I thank God that he didn't let the physical, emotional and mental abuse I suffered drive me into a mental institution. Because I serve a perfect God, He took my imperfections and made a beautiful woman out of me. I just want to let you know that it does not matter how messed up your past is, God is willing to give you another chance.

When I was going to high school, we sang a chorus during devotion - "Something wonderful, something good. All of my confusions, God understood. All I had to offer him was brokenness and pain but he made something beautiful out of my life."

I was never given a pulpit in sanctuaries for me to deliver my message to unsaved women, so I have ministered to them in laundry mats. Ladies, you would be surprised to know where God will allow you to minister to someone. I listen to women as they sit and do their laundry talking about their lives. Some of the stories I heard let me know that God was trying to get my attention so I could share my story with these ladies... in the laundry mat! As a result, I have used the opportunities to minister, encourage, and share my story with women to let them know that there is hope, and this hope is in Jesus.

I also visit domestic violence shelters letting women know about this hope. In my church, I find the broken and/or misunderstood and find a way to minister to them. I've seen women in need get ignored. The difficulties of my journey have allowed me to have a heart of compassion to those who are hurting and need a friend.

God did not have to keep me alive; He could have cut me off many times. But because of his infinite mercies towards me, He didn't. My children could have chosen drugs and alcohol as their route, but I thank God for keeping them. Ladies, I didn't think I had a purpose, but God showed me that I did and has allowed my life to be a testimony. I need you to make a choice to live, make a choice to live out your purpose despite everything you may be going through, and be true to yourself. Look in the mirror and ask yourself, "Who am I?" and don't be afraid to be you even with all of your scars, hurts, and pain. Remember that His grace is sufficient and His strength is made perfect in our weakness. Don't give up now! Better is coming! Your dreams and visions will come to pass! Expect the very best, and put no limitations on your life!

I thank God for allowing me to share my testimony with you. Everything may not apply to you, but I do hope that you find strength somewhere in the story. I am far from perfect, as I look to attain new strength in God every day. My desire is to be closer to Him as I continue on this journey. I want to live an exemplary life, and I want to continue to impact lives that I come in contact with. I am sometimes misunderstood, but please be patient with me because God is not through with me yet. When He's done, I shall come forth like pure gold. I will end with one of my favourite quotes: "I may not be where you would like me to be, but I am still in a better place than I was before."

Sharon Edmund-Brown is the mother of three beautiful children: Jessica, Jahmar and Jahron, and is a native of Jamaica. She currently resides in Paterson, New Jersey, where she is an active member of the True Witness Apostolic Church, which is referred to as the most exciting church in the tri-state area. Sharon enjoys singing on the choir and on the praise team, and is known as the True Witness Marvia Providence. She also enjoys ministering to women who have experiences similar to her own, and hopes to open a shelter to help domestic violence victims.

YOU CAN WIN
BY TRANESHA MARKS

Here I was... afraid, ashamed, broken, bitter, battered, wounded and torn. I had to decide to follow this God that I knew nothing about or stay in this hole, this pit of despair for the rest of my life. I asked myself: What if I'm searching for happiness that I'll never find? What if I don't like the person that I become in the process? What if the fire exposes too much? What if people realize that beneath all of this beauty, there's really just a little girl that wants to be free from being the puppet of reality? What if my choice to follow God was not a good decision? What if I never make the first step? What happens if I never try? Am I subconsciously choosing lack? If I never try, am I disqualifying myself from a life filled with peace, God's love, wealth and joy? Are we so afraid that we will miss God? Do we lack the courage to try Him?

Being a "God woman" in today's society is not necessarily the most popular choice. In fact, being a "God girl" sometimes doesn't seem worth it. Sometimes we feel like in choosing God we got the "short end of the stick" and it feels like God has left us alone to reap the results of our decision. Where do we turn when it feels like we are alone in the quest to live a life of righteousness? The world rejected us, it seems as if God isn't being fair to us, and it feels like we've failed ourselves. What happens when the picture that we painted of our Promised Land does not manifest? What happens when the business doesn't reach record breaking numbers? Who do we cry to when the ministry doesn't change as many lives as we expected? What if the marriage doesn't turn out to be the fairy tale that the wedding ceremony was? How do we continue to choose the life of a Godly woman when it seems like the life of a Godly woman is rejecting us?

James 1:3 declares: "For you know that when your faith is tested, your endurance has a chance to grow." We understand that through many tests and trials we eventually become the best version of who we are supposed to be. The hard part is trusting a process that appears to do more harm than good. There is nothing new under the sun.

There is no problem, no situation, and no circumstance that you will ever face that is new to God! We must learn not to allow our situations to dictate our faith. We must constantly dedicate our energy to positivity, to love, and to Christ! Remember that our faith must always overshadow our emotions. It is not about my feeling as if God is going to come through on my behalf; it is about believing the God to whom I dedicated my life. What I love about God is that He never allows us to catch anything by surprise. He never lied and said that we would not face persecution and He never said that we wouldn't have to suffer for choosing to walk with Him. When He said it, we just chose not to believe it. To many times as believers, we want to make God a superhero. We want Him to save us out of three feet of water that He has already trained us to swim in, instead of allowing God to be our master, our ruler, and our father. A wise father would never give anything to a child without them being tested and prepared for it. Our ability to withstand the process shows our love and respect for God. Do you love God enough to experience pain for His glory?

It's all about choosing to live a life that will be pleasing to God, even when choosing that life is no longer convenient. Today's God woman must understand the value of commitment. Learning to master the art of commitment has the power to keep us focused after we've lost our beginner's passion. Once life happens, a lot of times we choose to put our purpose on hold. Sometimes, we feel like it's better to stay stuck than to experience the pain that comes along with pursuing a life that we didn't initially ask for. We must learn to desire victory, even after defeats. You can still win.

You are God's woman. Everything that was meant to destroy you has built you. It has given you wisdom and power. There is power in learning how to stand after we've been knocked down. It's okay not having all the answers because we serve a God who created the problem and is the answer. Learn to trust that everything you need is found in God. If God is indeed our Creator, we must understand that He created everything concerning us as well. Our imperfections are made perfect in Christ.

We're hurt, we're broken, we experience turbulence and we get disappointed. Sometimes we're up and sometimes we're down. Sometimes we don't know which direction to go and sometimes we feel frozen. What do we do when the path of purpose seems to lead us nowhere? Who do we turn to when it seems as if we are the only ones in our lives truly seeking the plan of God? I have learned that it can be lonely when you feel like you are the only one who cares about seeking God's voice, His plan, and desires for our lives. As women, we have to fight through so much just to become our very own Proverbs 31 woman. Sometimes our hearts tell us to fight for who we love and other times we question if we even love what we're fighting for. We learn early that heartbreak must be a part of our resume, whether it is in love, in life, on our jobs, within our families, or even with ourselves. I've learned that it is in the crushing of our hearts that we have the ability to allow it to be made whole again through Christ. Each time we experience a blow, we have assurance that there is restoration in God. It is vital that we learn to allow nothing to separate us from the love of God. If God has control over everything, then what has the power to destroy us?

In the midst of your ability to trust God within the process, is the sureness of manifestation. Once God knows that He can trust us to carry the glory, there is nothing that we can't get God to do on our behalf. Without faith it is impossible to please God (Hebrews 11:6). But with faith, we have the power to move mountains!

I recall as a little girl my infatuation with the weather. Early in the morning, I'd turn on the television to check out the cool meteorologist to see what the day's forecast would be. Even though at times science proved itself wrong and the weather man falsely predicted forecasts, I still got up and trusted the meteorologist said about the weather. As I grew older, I asked myself, why don't I trust God the way I did the meteorologists? God has never been wrong, He has never failed and He has never incorrectly predicted the weather. Why is it so hard to believe that all of the storms in our lives are being masterfully controlled by the Chief Meteorologist? Is it so hard to believe that what God is saying concerning our lives is true because it sounds too good?

Once we learn to change the way we view ourselves, it becomes much easier for us to experience life. Everything that you face is only a by-product of who you are. If we could all learn to walk in and embrace our greatness, we would quickly begin to see the hand of God working in our lives and in the lives of those around us. We must accept the challenge to boldly trust all of the ingredients that are working in our lives. Commitment says that no matter what I see, I know that this will all work together so that the glory of God may be revealed in my life. It is not about me being perfect, but it is more about my ability to stay committed to the plan of God and to acknowledge that my purpose in God is the only plan that will ever yield Godly manifestation.

One of the best things that I have ever done was connecting to the right people. I learned early in life that being properly connected to the people that God has placed in our lives, and understanding the season and the timing of the people in our lives, will always produce fruit. We cannot be afraid to cut the cord of those that have served their purpose in our lives. Society makes us believe that parting ways is such a bad thing. There can be no resurrection without the parting of Judas. There must be a separation of some sort in your life, whether it's from people that loved you or people that have betrayed you. Jesus was on the cross alone. There was a separation, a parting from even those that followed Him to the cross. But we understand that the separation produced life. Separation does not always imply that people are bad for us. Sometimes it simply implies that they have served their purpose in our lives for that particular season. Connections can either hinder us or bless us. It is up to us to find out what purpose our connections serve.

Mary and Elizabeth are often used to describe the power of connection. I often wonder what would have happened had Mary connected herself to someone other than Elizabeth, or vice versa. It is important to fill divine covenant positions with the right people because the wrong connections can cost you. Are your positions of divine covenant already filled? Are they qualified by God or are they simply entertainment for your flesh? Seek God about the connections in your life so that everyone that surrounds you serves a God purpose in every area of your life.

In our walk with God, we must understand that it is completely fine to fix ourselves before we try to fix anyone else. Your team benefits from you being 100% healthy. Although the Romans 15:1 says, "We who are strong ought to bear with the failings of the weak," imagine how much more powerful the body could be if we all developed our strengths as well as our weaknesses. We would be invincible. Sometimes we get so busy and so overwhelmed with the pressure to make the game winning shot that we neglect preparation for the game. The preparation is just as important, if not more important, as the performance. You matter. Your heart and your well-being matter. Your role in the play is to be taken just as serious as the people that you are performing for. Your desire to please God must exceed your desire to please man. We must be willing to take time out of our busy lives to petition the throne of God for instructions concerning our lives. A team is only as strong as its weakest player. Your provision will be located in your ability to agree with the plan of God concerning your life. Oneness with God is important simply because it will allow you to locate the areas in your life that need to be shaped and molded. Once we allow God to prune and purge us, then we are prepared to see the blessings of God reign in our lives.

A lot of times our dreams and visions never manifest because they are our dreams and not God's. Wherever God guides, He will always provide. The Bible declares in Matthew 25:23, that if we learn to be faithful over a few things, God will make us ruler over many things.

However, there can be no promotion if we are faithful over the wrong stuff. We must quit watering the wrong seed and expecting it to bring forth fruit. Some of us need to go back and re-believe God, but this time for the promise He made to us and not the promise that we chose to make ourselves. A lot of times, we struggle in life because we never consulted God about our battles. It is simply a matter of us fighting for the wrong stuff. Our plan may work for a moment, but God's plan for our lives has the ability to impact our bloodlines for generations to come. Good things do not always equate to the substance and the power of a God thing. If it seems as if everything in your life came very natural for you, there's a great chance that you are not operating in the power of purpose. If you did not need God to achieve the success that you have attained, most likely it is not God who blessed you. The enemy confuses a lot of our success stories by making us believe that just because something works in our favor it must mean that God agrees with it. God is not interested in fighting against our wills. However, your good thing has no power to compare to the great thing that God desires to have for your life. Be prayerful of all things. Life is too valuable to settle for the counterfeit lifestyle because we have convinced ourselves to believe that the promised lifestyle was not worth the effort. We are not perfect but we can be made whole in Christ. No matter the journey to wholeness, we know that if God is the pilot that we will always make it to our destinations safely.

    I was in my car listening to Pandora and a song came on that I had never heard before. It was "Pieces" by Tamar. At this point in my life, I was living in my car. I had exhausted all of my options. I had run to every person I could. I had cried on every shoulder possible and I was exhausted. I was tired of running. I had nowhere else to go. At my dead end, God spoke to me. It was a place He needed me. Right at the end of the song, I heard Tamar say: "I want the whole thing; don't forget about me". True enough I heard Tamar, but I also heard a much louder voice; I heard God through Tamar's vocals telling me that He did not want just half of me, that He wanted all of me.

    That moment changed the course of my life. I gave God the heaviness that I had been carrying for years and the hurts that I had been covering up as early as my childhood. I told Him the truth and I asked Him for forgiveness. I needed Him to forgive me, but I needed Him to help me forgive myself. Here I was a beautiful, gifted, talented, anointed, and powerful woman... sleeping in my car. I was so low. I felt like everyone in my life had abandoned me but it was in that moment that God found me. I was a broken, beaten, washed up, tired, patched up, and patted down refuge with a bruised heart and skewed vision. God found me. I was overwhelmed with emotions as tears streamed down my face but such a comfort came over me. After everyone else walked out, God stepped in. After everyone else had their say, God had the final say! He told me that I was not a handful, He said nothing the enemy told me was true. He told me that He love me. It was in that moment that I realized the power of love. It was love that saved me, love that freed me and love that delivered me. I vowed to God that I would forever spread the entity that set me free.

Know that God's plan for your life is bigger than everything that you may be facing. Nothing the enemy does has power to counter what God has already said. You deserve everything that God has the power to give you. Like me, you can be free. You can choose life and you can choose to be whole. You are super. You are beautiful. You are amazing. Don't give up the fight because you can win.

Tranesha Marks is a dynamic speaker, teacher, leader, change agent and purpose coach. She desires to inspire, motivate and encourage a generation to embrace purpose, choose destiny and follow God. Tranesha currently resides in Baton Rouge, La and is the founder of ABL coaching, a company she began in 2013, that focuses on aiding others in walking in purpose. She is striving to change the nature of a generation and help to lead a lost generation back to Christ.

LOST AND FOUND IN THE BALANCE
BY KANISHA ANDERSON

"Kanisha, where does your confidence come from?"

The question caught me off guard. It wasn't something I expected walking in a semi-busy mall on a sunny, spring Saturday afternoon. We were talking and laughing about the things we normally talk and laugh about. Life experiences, funny stories and the daily happenings in our lives and the world. Even as someone I know pretty well, Taylor's question seemingly came out of nowhere. Just a few seconds ago, we were talking about something completely different.

"My confidence?" I asked.

"Yeah. You seem so confident in who you are as a person. Where does it come from?" Taylor replied.

Before jumping into my response, I carefully gave it thought. On the surface level, it's a simple answer: I worked hard to become the woman I am today. I constantly and consciously pushed myself towards wholeness and balance. Through adversity, I worked hard to create successful patterns in my professional career, spiritual walk, academic achievements, and my character. That wasn't difficult to share. Explaining *how* I did that work, however, proved a little more complicated.

With the conversation I thought we were having now obviously in the past, I looked at the person asking me the question. Observing

Taylor's body language, I analyzed where I believe the question stemmed from. It wasn't sheer curiosity. I'm not a psychologist nor have I extensively studied psychology or psychotherapy. Well, at least, nothing beyond an extremely labour-intensive, first year university course. However, it's a well-known fact that you can learn a lot about someone if you analytically observe his or her body language. What they say, how they say it, when, where and why. I listened and noted the inquisitive tone in their voice, but saw and evaluated the averted gaze, avoiding eye contact. Clearly, Taylor didn't need or want a cliché response. I could tell Taylor was on a journey, searching and needing a guiding answer.

"Well...," Though it appeared I was unsure, I knew exactly how I would respond. It's not a difficult question for me. It's an easy answer, but I knew I couldn't give the easy answer without an explanation. Knowing what Taylor was really asking and needing; I had to paint a Jean-Michel. "Truthfully," I continued, "it's been a journey that many people don't really hear because I don't usually share it." The eyes that previously avoided eye contact during the initial questioning now locked with mine in anticipation. "Confidence can be so easily misunderstood, but I definitely don't mind sharing my story with you."

I was born and raised in church. At the very least, throughout my childhood, adolescence and young adulthood, nearly every Sunday was spent in church. Excluding a few brief periods during university, I had no problem with that. I loved church and since I attended the same church until my early 20's, it naturally felt like a spiritual home. I saw the same people week after week, even as new faces increasingly populated the congregation. Most importantly, there were many youth and children in my church, several of which are still there. People I watched evolve from toddlers, to children, from teenagers to young adults, at the same time as me. The home where I grew up, I saw my church as a "spiritual haven" filled with those who upheld the same core values I did.

At school I had friends and blended well with people from every social group and race. On a surface level, I could connect with various groups and avoided boxed-in categories that defined who I could and couldn't connect with. Although my upbringing somewhat ingrained a belief that I should separate myself from the "world", even as a Christian, this was my "social home". I always knew I was "different", but that didn't hold me back from befriending and loving my non-Christian peers. As a kid, I loved school. If church was the essential "spiritual haven", where I connected with those who shared my beliefs, school was the "social haven", where I flourished.

I should probably mention that even in childhood, my life always hinged on balance, namely between my religion and, really, everything else. That's not to say I compromised my beliefs or my values. Even though I made mistakes, there are ideas and principles secularism embraces that a Christian must reject. However, I grew up in a church environment that explicitly and implicitly advocated extremism. Separation from the world, in speech, behaviour, dress, attitudes and perspective was an honour badge. Separation in every way, with your religious beliefs as the core motivation, indicated how committed you were to God and your spiritual development. It's not that I didn't believe separation on some level was important; I just couldn't subscribe to the extremism. Outside church, I grew up in a balanced home environment that truly, blended the best of both worlds. This balance helped define my character and the older I was, the more I cherished it.

As I entered my adolescence, I started feeling like I watched life through a paradoxical "looking glass". In both my "spiritual" and "social havens", I interacted with others, engaged in conversations, and shared experiences. However, deep down, I started feeling like I really didn't belong. I participated, but simultaneously watched from the outside looking in. I grew up feeling like the team player that's in the game, but isn't quite a part of the team. Although I was still well liked and respected, the strain of being different grew and intensified. I never tried to be the same as everyone else, but as everyone seemed to pursue one path, I was committed to staying on mine. Partially due to my religious upbringing, I wasn't interested in some of the things my peers wanted to do. I didn't really judge them; we had different interests when it came to certain things and I was uninterested in compromising. Moreover, my mother wanted to keep me safe *and* saved at ALL times, which usually meant overprotection.

Further compounding the matter, I felt left out with what was going on in my friends' lives. Within our small crew, I started feeling and being excluded, especially during the last half of grade 11 and all of grade 12. Increasingly, I looked at what was once a haven, as a foreign home where I was no longer welcome. I analyzed my friendships and my social circles, comparing the happy image social fulfillment once posed and the growing stark contrast my current reality presented. I knew I wasn't perfect, but no one on this planet could make that claim. I couldn't understand why there was no longer a place where I could authentically and genuinely connect.

The "spiritual haven" was a little different. Ironically, although I was well known and respected in the "social haven", at church I was never in the "in crowd". I existed on the fringes. Frankly, I was never interested in being an "all about church, but completely separated from the world" Christian I saw so often in church circles. However, as I hit middle school, I definitely didn't see a place for me. When I hit high school and I started learning about the world, and myself truthfully, I lost the desire to connect with any one on any level. In my mind, I still somewhat had a "social haven", and I was cool with the connections I already possessed. I felt ignored and didn't care if I was seen. At 16, in my mind it was, 'Yeah okay, there's the church thing and that's important, but I want to discuss more about life. Tell me about the world and how you see it.' I wanted to know how they felt about the world and social issues, not just living in the Christian bubble religion imposed upon us. Along with feeling ignored, I sought balance in others around me and just couldn't see it.

It didn't help that I was very quiet which made onlookers think I was stuck up. What no one understood was I wasn't quiet because I was rude, I was quiet because I felt surrounded by strangers I grew up with. It wasn't until around the time I graduated from high school and started coming more into my own, that people started checking for me. Even though I grew up in that church, I began feeling like I had nothing in common with anyone aside from how you become and stay a Christian. On a large scale, although I managed to create a few friendships, I didn't belong. Eventually I saw most as super-churchy, someone all about church and the church realm, poorly connecting with the outside world. On the surface I became jaded, not caring if I was visible or not. However deep down, it created a huge internal struggle. Although I thought the "social haven" was important, I wanted to connect, and stay connected in the "spiritual haven" as well. In the end, I always felt excluded, unwelcome to the social clubs and cliques. So eventually, I came to terms with feeling invisible in my own home.

As time passed, my inability to find a place where I belonged increased, and though I longed for it, I stopped searching. What do you do as a Christian when you feel out of place in your "church world"? What's the solution when you feel well liked and known in the "world", but you can never fully belong, because you're called to be different? Where do you go when you hang in the balance, but need a foundation? Although I had a few friends here and there, that's completely different from feeling and knowing where you belong. In response, I steadily grew into myself. Discouraged from exclusion, I was determined "to be my own best friend". Even still, I felt an increasing paradox growing within me. I was tired of feeling like an outsider. I was tired of getting hurt in friendships. I longed for companionship, but preferred my own space. I knew it wasn't healthy to be alone, and truth be told I hated it, but my isolation at least guaranteed one thing. If I was alone, I couldn't get hurt. Though this was all true, the loneliness in feeling out of place overpowered me at times. I built barriers to prevent hurt from others, but I was hurting within the barriers because I needed connectivity.

For years, this paradox drove me crazy. My internal thought process was "I don't fit in, so I won't bother, but I'm lonely and I hate it". There were times where I felt like my loneliness was so overwhelming it was tangible. In the middle of a packed crowd I would feel absolutely alone and isolated. I had great support from my family, particularly from my mother and aunt. Their wisdom seemingly knows no boundaries. An almost intrinsic level of discernment and wisdom, they showed me how to grow and mature, while balancing logic and spirituality. They were and, will always be, God-given compasses. Even though I appreciated and needed their support, I longed for connections with my peers. Truthfully, I spent a very long time praying to God from within my protective walls, asking Him to fill that void. I wanted a place where my piece would finally fit into a puzzle. I prayed and spent years looking in earnest expectation, awaiting my answered prayers. However, as the years passed, and no solution came, I accepted idea of being alone.

As a naturally private person, I often prefer to deal with issues myself before sharing with others. Although I'm like this with nearly everyone, there are times where I can acknowledge I need to share my burden. During one of my many heart-to-hearts with my mother, I expressed my disdain for feeling like I didn't fit in anywhere. I tried to get comfortable with it, but loneliness isn't really a comforting feeling. Never one to veer into much self-pity, she asked me a question I never previously considered. "You prayed that God would change your situation. Have you ever asked God why He has you in it? Obviously there's a reason for everything. Find the purpose." This simple question ignited a radical shift in my perspective. After searching for that "belonging place", I realized I needed to switch from "God I need you to change this" to "God I want to know why". I grew tired and honestly, slightly impatient asking God to plant me in another "haven". I started looking at things differently, realizing He had the answer I needed. I embarked on a journey in God, not only to receive an answer, but also discover myself in finding and immersing myself in Him. Although I always aimed to maintain strong self-awareness, one can very easily feel unimportant, unvalued and invisible when you don't feel like you belong anywhere. In seeking God, I learned why He kept me hanging on that balancing line.

The more I discovered God, His purpose and myself, the more I learned about my identity in Him. That all-encompassing isolation pushed and propelled me to find God amidst my painful reality. My isolation was the funneling force that pushed me into God-recovery and self-discovery. I learned my purpose and from there discovered my value. Moreover, and most importantly, I saw God's permeating presence throughout my life. During times where I felt the most alone, isolated and segregated from everyone, His comfort and presence was the strongest. I still believe and know that social connection is imperative to human psychological growth and development. However, during those times I saw God's faithfulness in staying near me, as long as I stayed near Him.

Life itself is an anthology. Every life stage is a volume, every major life curve creates a chapter, and every minor life turn enhances the plot. I probably sat down to write this piece almost a dozen times before I actually started. Before I sat down those 12 times, I must have asked myself double that amount what I would even write about. It's not that I don't have a story.

I'm not 30 yet, but a few chapters of my life could be expanded into books, with sequels and subsequent film adaptations. Every life is a story. Even if it's not the most dramatic, it's important. Telling one's story, whatever the plot requires transparency, honesty, and comfort in sharing it with others. We all have something in common: our lives are anthologies with permanent entries co-authored by yourself, your life-shaping experiences and God's plan. Our stories weave narratives that collectively beautify our humanity. Regardless of how dark, bright, tragic or joyful, your story is one of the few things in this world that without fail distinguishes you from everyone else.

In searching for a home where I belonged, I found God and in God I found my destiny, identity and value. That's what makes my story and journey beautiful. Nothing can empower you more than finding yourself in God. There's no higher level of knowledge, than discovering the inner most parts of yourself after delving deeper into a relationship with your Creator. In my searching, I found a foundation and on that foundation I built every aspect of my personhood. This world is full of ideologies, perspectives and voices that try to show you who you are and what you should be, where you should belong and where you shouldn't. Assigned categories based on behaviour, attitudes and beliefs, and they're quite believable too. The truth is only God can give you that revelation.

It wasn't until I became a youth leader in my church that I fully realized the purpose of my experience. I love all the young people in my church. However, my eye is particularly keen on seeing those who don't fit into the "in crowd". The young people who feel like they're invisible in their own church, knowing they aren't like most peers at school, searching for their place in the world, but unsure of how to find it. The youth who know that they've been called to be different, but feel like being alone isn't worth the struggle, and contemplate whether it's worth the compromise. The one who feels like they never belonged and subsequently struggle with feeling inadequate and unimportant. I strongly care about those who feel like loneliness has been a better companion than most of the friends they've had in their lifetime. My experience brought me to and through a place that enables me to look at others and confidently tell them you are not alone. You are valuable and even if you have to stand alone, your destiny is still packed with power and purpose.

After years of feeling unimportant and invisible, I know I'm not. The confidence that keeps my head up when I walk, gracefully crafts my speech when I speak and fuels my motivation for the future comes from this story. My confidence doesn't come from the things I accomplished. I appreciate the post-secondary degrees, the past jobs, and the set and achieved goals. However, like the rushing river current streaming under the top frozen layer, they don't fully exhibit who I am. I achieved those things because I know myself. I learned how much I matter, and how much I'm needed in this world. I needed to make God my haven, not human social circles. I needed to define myself through His perspective and see myself the way He did. In my journey I learned a truth I can share with others. I built myself on this foundation and I can look to those who feel the same way I did, and confidently say you are not invisible. You matter and this world needs your presence.

Kanisha Elizabeth Anderson was born and raised in suburban Toronto. She sums up her passion in three words: God, people and life. Her life's mission is to showcasing the real, loving God; authentically connect with different people; and live a joyful, successful and purposeful life.

ABOUT SISTERS IN PRAISE

"See, I have this day set thee over the nations and over the kingdoms, to root out, and to pull down, and to destroy, and to... throw down, to build, and to plant." Jeremiah 1:10

Sisters In Praise is for young women who are hungry for God. This is a prayer based group, as we realize that nothing we do in this world can be done without the foundation of prayer. Sisters In Praise, also known as, "Godly Women Pray," meet for prayer every Tuesday at 5 am and Thursday at 8:30 pm via conference call. This group of young women are committed to seeking the face of God and growing in Him. This group enables and fosters spiritual growth for each young woman who joins through activating spiritual gifts, finding purpose, and much more.

Although we cater to younger women, we are not limited to this one category. Sisters In Praise endeavors to impact and inspire the lives of women all over the world.

We are a faith-based group which believes in the death, burial and resurrection of Jesus Christ.

Follow Sisters in Praise:
www.SistersinPraise.ca
Twitter - @SistersinPraise
Facebook – https://www.facebook.com/pages/Sisters-in-Praise/1606542399577712

FOR MORE TITLES FROM EX3 BOOKS

VISIT OUR WEBSITE AT:
www.EX3ent.com

Feel free to share your reviews of
JOURNEYS OF GODLY WOMEN
via our website, email
ExpectedEndEntertainment@gmail.com, or on Amazon.com.

www.ingramcontent.com/pod-product-compliance
Lightning Source LLC
Chambersburg PA
CBHW070503100426
42743CB00010B/1737